THE
UNDERGROUND
☞ GUIDE TO ☜
UNIVERSITY STUDY
IN BRITAIN AND
IRELAND

THE
UNDERGROUND
☞ GUIDE TO ☜
UNIVERSITY STUDY
IN BRITAIN AND
IRELAND

BILL GRIESAR

INTERCULTURAL PRESS, INC.

For information, contact:
Intercultural Press, Inc.
P.O. Box 700
Yarmouth, ME 04096, USA

Book design by Jacques Chazaud.
Cover design by LetterSpace.
Printed in the United States of America.

97 96 95 94 93   2 3 4 5 6

Library of Congress Cataloging-in-Publication Data

Griesar, Bill.
    The underground guide to university study in Britain and Ireland/
Bill Griesar.
        p.   cm.
    Includes bibliographical references (p.   ).
    ISBN 1-877864-03-X
    1. Foreign study—Great Britain.   2. Foreign study—Ireland.
3. American students—Great Britain.   4. American students—
Ireland.
    I. Title.
    LB2376.3.G7G75   1992
    370.19'6'0941—dc20   91-45425
                                                                    CIP

Contents

3. Before Leaving and upon Arrival

4. What to Expect

5. Social and Cultural Issues

6. Transportation

7. Money and Banking

8. Health

9. Communication

10. Sports

11. Entertainment and the Media

Foreword

A s a foreign study advisor for over twenty years, I've adhered to several principles, one of which is "full information first." It has been my experience that the more information students applying for foreign study have available to them, the more capable they are of choosing the best location for their goals and the more successful they will be during their sojourn.

When Bill Griesar's initial prospectus first came to me in 1988, I subjected it to the late Lily von Klemperer's criteria for evaluating study abroad literature found in her classic pamphlet, "How to Read Study Abroad Literature." The proposal passed with flying colors. In my enthusiastic response I noted some suggestions and also wrote, "When your work is published, I would expect it to find rapid and wide acceptance among foreign study advisors and undergraduates."

Nothing has changed my mind. In its final version, *The Underground Guide to University Study in Britain and Ireland* includes virtually everything an American or Canadian student planning to study in England, Ireland, Wales, or Scotland would want to know. In a humorous, easy-to-read, and straightforward style, Bill Griesar addresses virtually every aspect of a student's experience: where, how, and when to apply; what to do about prescriptions and luggage; how to hitchhike; what foods to try; and how to cope with culture shock and why it occurs. The author also covers popular sports, resources for the disabled, classroom and academic strategies, multicultural issues, and much more. Bill's zest for his subject comes through on every page; yet his ebullience in no way obscures the seriousness or accuracy of what is presented. His extensive set of appendixes is informative and sometimes entertaining, particularly the colorful vocabulary lists in appendix C.

It is clear to those of us in international educational exchange that Bill has done his homework. Rather than relying primarily on information from British and Irish institutions themselves or on his own experiences studying at Sussex University, Griesar returned to the area to conduct interviews with over one hundred North American and Canadian students who were currently studying or who had studied in Great Britain or Ireland. He discovered what students felt were the most important issues to cover: what they wished they had been told, what they thought they would need but didn't, what they hadn't expected.

In response to their comments and observations, Bill has compiled information that would otherwise need to be culled from several different sources and, in many cases, information that was previously unavailable.

This volume comes at an important time in the foreign study community. British and Irish universities have adapted many of their processes and information sources to answer the needs and queries of Americans. Also, national studies are calling for more foreign experience for American students; for example, "Educating for Global Competence: The Report of the Advisory Council for International Educational Exchange" has called for a substantial increase in study abroad numbers, and for placing high priority in our institutions on developing international awareness and providing an education that prepares students for an interdependent competitive world.

The Underground Guide provides abundant information while encouraging and facilitating the study abroad process in a manner easily accessible to students. As such it is a valuable tool for promoting broader cultural understanding and international competence for North American graduates.

Robbins Winslow
Director, Educational Services (Foreign Study)
Trinity College, Hartford, CT

Acknowledgments

R esearching this book was a huge project. I would like to take this opportunity to express my sincere thanks to the many who helped me along the way: Bob Duehmig, for researching Irish universities, for hitchhiking above and beyond the call of duty (and his Fulbright bosses, who almost called out the guard), for providing excellent advice on all things Irish and on the Guide in general, and for living on pizza and Guinness in pursuit of publication; Katherine Dyar, who used her journalistic abilities to research and write up the first draft of chapter 8, Health; Noelle Sweeney, who scoured the offices of Skill and other organizations in search of information on help for the disabled; Matt Cruice and Karen Guttentag, sports experts, for explaining everything from football to rugby; Fiona Green for her friendship, her couch, and her roasts; Jan Finn, Steve Alty, Kim Couzens, John Attridge, Catherine Boyle, Sarah Richardson, Alison Corbett, Margaret Turner, Claire, and Captain John Franklin of the Fulbright Commission in London for friendship and for advice on everything from cricket to the Barley Mow; Gerry Thompson, Jim Gillis, Michael Oliver, Nicky Sawicki, Mark Edwards,

Kevin Smalls, Jörgen Dyer, Margit Tucker, Marie Ericsson, Steve Musham, Val Reid, and Colin Speakman at the American Institute for Foreign Study, and particularly Gerry Thompson, Jim Gillis, Val Reid, and Colin Speakman, who arranged for an office for me in London; Robbins Winslow of Trinity College Office of Educational Services (Foreign Study) for initial funding and subsequent advice; Peggy Stone-Cox, David Larsen, and Will Migniuolo at the Beaver College Center for Education Abroad for their support and for arranging housing in London dorms for twenty-one months of research abroad; Franz Jost at International Student Exchange Flights, who provided transatlantic transport in order to get this whole project started; Robin Hickey, Edel Kinsel, and everyone on staff at Kinlay House in Dublin for arranging five months of housing, support, insight into Ireland, and many good pints of Guinness; Mr. and Mrs. Colcord for housing in London; John Pearson, Nigel Rogers, Mike Woolf, Mike Masterson, Mike Reddin, Lorna Stern, Adrienne Wong, and the Intercultural Press for much welcome editing and spirited advice; and finally, thanks to my family for all of their support.

THE
UNDERGROUND
☞ GUIDE TO ☜
UNIVERSITY STUDY
IN BRITAIN AND
IRELAND

1

Study Abroad

WHY STUDY ABROAD?

Over 12,000 North Americans travel overseas each year to study at one of the forty-eight universities, thirty polytechnics, fourteen central institutions, and eight regional technical colleges in Britain and Ireland. Why do they go? "To experience a new way of life." "I want to study abroad, but in an English-speaking country." "My grandfather's from Scotland, and we have relatives over there." "I want to study Welsh literature, so Bangor seems like the place." "I want to study U.S. history, and I'll bet the English have unique opinions on that." "Why, I'm Irish myself!" But the most common reason is neatly expressed by one American spending a year at Bristol: "I was fed up with school and wanted a change of pace." Many hope to escape another year at home; they want to travel, experience a new culture, and make friends abroad. You will definitely experience this "change of pace"—and a lot more. When you study abroad, you don't just travel to a new country, you live in that country and must adapt to the culture. Living in Ireland or Britain means trading a familiar set of joys and woes for a new set, and attending school abroad will plunge you into a foreign educational system that is different in every respect.

While study abroad is certainly time off from stateside school, it is also intense and rewarding and requires plenty of work. You don't just study, research, write, and hand in essays as you did at SUNY Albany, Northwestern, or Berkeley. You've got to figure out how to use the banks, the money, the telephones, and the postal system. You must adjust to the climate and culture and, yes, even learn to speak the language of your temporarily adopted home. Some North Americans choose Britain and Ireland because "they're so similar to the U.S. or Canada," but in fact it's only a superficial similarity, and subtle and not-so-subtle differences frequently trip you up. What will you think when you're feeling low those first few weeks and your British friend tells you to "keep your pecker up?" What if you don't understand your Glaswegian (from Glasgow) roommate? How do you play cricket, and why are some students such fanatical fans? Why do people act so strangely? Where's the textbook for your politics course and why is the suggested reading list a hundred pages long? Study abroad requires full-time attention, because unless you lock yourself away with other North Americans and refuse to believe you're overseas, you can't escape being a newcomer who's got to work at learning the rules, expectations, history, and heroes of a very different place. This is as true in Britain and Ireland as it would be in Mexico, France, or Indonesia. All of this will cause some confusion, frazzled nerves, headaches, and frustration—in other words, culture shock (see chapter 5 for more information on culture shock).

You will certainly learn a lot about Britain and Ireland. You might not go around advising people to keep their pecker up, but you'll know what it means, and maybe cricket won't be as unintelligible or boring as it first appeared. You'll gain confidence in yourself, trust yourself to take on new risks and responsibilities, and people won't seem so strange after all. "It's ironic," notes one British lecturer, "that students from "the land of rugged individualism" are often pampered and sheltered in their own country and really grow up over here." You'll gain independence after cooking and caring for yourself. "I couldn't make toast before I came. I also didn't realize that toast is about the best food you can get in this country, or that people put beans on it!" You'll travel a lot, but not just a two-week, whirlwind European Eurail tour. You'll be able to slow down and see and appreciate more of what you are experiencing. You'll learn to avoid the "I've got to see every church and museum and hit Bath Friday, Edinburgh Saturday, and the Outer Hebrides during the week" syndrome. You'll gain perspective, too. Students say they learn as much about North America as they do about Ireland and Britain, as much about themselves as about the Irish and British. Those from the U.S. see their country viewed critically from abroad and often join intense conversations about politics and culture. "I went to the union bar and had to defend our Central American and Middle Eastern policies for over an hour. Students really know about international affairs." And finally, you'll experience the excitement and pleasure of becoming part of an overseas campus community, meeting and making friends, studying your subject under a new system, and becoming a little bit Irish, English, Welsh, or Scottish yourself. The result is a lot of healthy self-assessment, change, and growth. And this kind of learning goes on not only in the classrooms but also around the kitchen table, in the dining hall, in the pub, and elsewhere.

WHAT SORT OF STUDY ABROAD?

Once you've made the decision to study in Ireland or Britain, there are several other questions to consider.

How Long?

You can go abroad for four weeks to four years. Short stays can be exhilarating but, compared to longer study, superficial and incomplete. You will not be in Britain or Ireland long enough to get to know people. You'll see some sights, attend a few lectures, and visit a couple of museums and pubs, but you won't be able to explore the culture in any great depth. When you get home, you might pay greater attention to articles on Dublin or televised newsbreaks from Birmingham and Bath, but you won't have developed that close link with the country that comes from living there for an extended period. Students choosing longer stays seem to feel more satisfied, learn more from their studies, gain deeper insight into the culture, and make closer friends. Some British and Irish universities (for example, Trinity College, Bristol, Durham, and St. Andrews) won't even allow you to enroll for less than a full academic year. While many legitimate institutions will let you in for shorter periods, be wary of programs called "study breaks" or "study tours" that seem especially short (e.g., eight weeks or less). They may emphasize the "break" or the "tour" far more than

the "study." It's cheaper and just as rewarding to take some time off
and go traveling instead.

Many North American students head to Britain and Ireland on a
junior year abroad (JYA), as a supplement to their regular degree
course at home. One term (about twelve weeks) in the autumn, two
terms (eighteen weeks) in the spring and summer, or a full year (thirty
weeks) are the most common options. While this overseas study
usually takes place during junior year, some students will go abroad
as sophomores or seniors.

Where?

You can choose the traffic and historical wealth of Glasgow or the
natural beauty and solitude of the Irish Galway coast. Students in
large cities praise the convenience and multitude of cultural activities, from theaters and museums to zoos and shops. There are
extensive subway *(underground)* and above-ground transportation
systems in Newcastle, Liverpool, London, Glasgow, and Dublin, which
can make it a lot easier to get around. Yet, a city can be alienating and
a difficult place to make friends. Smaller communities can be closer
and more friendly but also more claustrophobic.

Language is another consideration. Traveling from county to
county (let alone country to country) will expose you to a range of
accents and vocabulary. You'll get used to all varieties of English in
due course, although in some parts of Wales (especially the northwest), Welsh is more popular, and Irish (or *Gaeilge*) is a common
language near Galway.

The size of the university is also an important consideration. Would
you feel more comfortable at a large institution, which offers more
courses and facilities than a small college but might seem overwhelm-
ing and impersonal? British and Irish universities generally have
fewer students than the average college in Canada or the States.
Nothing approaching the 60,000 at Toronto or Ohio State! The range
is from about 750 at tiny St. David's to over 10,000 at Birmingham,
Manchester, Nottingham, and Leeds.

Also think about the number of North Americans each school or city
is likely to attract. Keep in mind that it's much easier to meet British
and Irish students when you're on your own. You are likely to have a
more genuine cross-cultural experience in less tourist-visited, cam-
era-clogged spots. Some universities recruit too many students from
the United States and Canada, and some cities (especially London,

Edinburgh, and Dublin) are deluged by North Americans and visitors
from around the globe, so locals may be less inclined to meet you.

What Kind of Program?

You can go abroad with a U.S. university or study abroad organization that arranges housing; sets up your bank account; launders your
sheets; transfers your credits; budgets your money; enables your
parents to reach you; tells you how to buy clothes, get a haircut, find
a birthday cake, and generally runs your life. For some students who
want to be helped through every step, this is the only way to go. Others
are more gung-ho individuals who, with a letter of acceptance from a
British or Irish university in hand, will strap backpack to shoulders
and figure on buying a toothbrush overseas. Between these extremes
are a multitude of programs to suit every need.

It is helpful to develop a set of questions to ask advisors or program
representatives when considering going abroad through your own or
another university. The following will help you get started:

Is this program fully integrated? You learn more when you live
with the British and Irish students and take the same classes. Ask if you
will be in the same dormitories as the Irish/British, if there will be
separate classes for North American students, if the classes will be
taught by Irish/British lecturers. Find out if you are expected to join
regular meetings or excursions arranged by the program (many
students claim that such "outings" detract from their experience by
separating them from the local students).

Are there any course restrictions? Sometimes a university or study
abroad program won't allow North Americans to take certain classes
(mostly science) or make use of particular facilities (mostly labs).
North American students generally must have the appropriate background for each British or Irish course they'd like to take. In particular, if you plan to pursue courses in languages or science, it helps
if you've taken a few related classes before applying overseas (see
chapter 4, "What to Expect").

What does the price include? Ask about tuition and whether the
fees are higher for science courses as opposed to arts courses (this is
often the case). Is housing included? Meals? Local transportation,
student identity cards, any special orientation programs or

homestays? Are there offices in London, Edinburgh, Cardiff, or Dublin—people you can reach for advice? Will financial aid be transferable? Are there additional sources of funding?

What about credit transfer? Probably the best (and some say only) reason for choosing an organized study abroad program over direct application is the peace of mind that comes from knowing that somebody will likely be aware of your academic progress and can contact both the overseas institution and your home college about the transfer of credit. If you apply directly, you'll have to make your own arrangements with the advisors and faculty (see page 8, "Apply Directly," for more information).

What services for overseas students are offered by the university? Some British and Irish universities have advisors who deal specifically with North American students, but many do not. If the university you choose already offers extensive counseling and expertise with credit transfer and other concerns, a program may not be necessary at all.

Does the institution allow admission for single terms? Many universities require a commitment of at least two terms of enrollment.

Is the program reliable and capably run? Ask your study abroad advisor, department chair, or registrar about past dealings with any programs you are considering.

Can this program accommodate the needs of disabled students? If you are disabled, the news is not good. Although the United States has passed landmark legislation dramatically expanding access for the disabled, attitudes and practices of the U.K. and Irish governments are behind the times. Even universities built in the 1960s often lack elevators *(lifts)* and ramps, while older universities offer fewer facilities (to be fair, it's not easy to adapt sixteenth-century buildings for disabled access). Be aware that Britain and Ireland require animals (including seeing-eye dogs) to be kept in quarantine for six months to prevent the import of rabies, unknown in these islands. Nevertheless, if you're keen to make it overseas, you can overcome any obstacles in your way. Here are some ideas that may help in planning your study abroad:

1. Start early! Before you decide to attend a university, research their facilities to determine which can accommodate your needs. Find out what adaptations the university is prepared to make and at whose cost.

2. Don't presume anything. Check whether accessibility and safety measures are up to scratch, support services adequate, special equipment available, housing appropriate, and specific exam conditions adequate.

3. See appendix A for contacts which can assist you in this process.

4. When you apply, describe your disability and special requirements in detail.

HOW TO STUDY ABROAD FOR A SEMESTER OR A YEAR

If your university has a study abroad office (and/or advisor), that is the first place to visit. Some study abroad offices have a library of material, including catalogs and guidebooks to help you decide how and where to go. Your advisor might know about your options and have specific suggestions on programs or universities that are right for you. If there is no official advisor, perhaps a faculty member is responsible for students considering study overseas. See your own personal academic advisor and/or chair of your department, either of whom may have information on your options or suggestions on how to proceed. Also check your college bookstore for books on international study opportunities. You can write for catalogs and pamphlets from organizations that publish material dealing with study abroad, including the Institute of International Education (IIE), the Council on International Educational Exchange (CIEE), NAFSA, the Association of International Educators, and Intercultural Press. Consult appendix A for a list of addresses.

There are three main ways to study abroad: you may apply through your own university, through another university, or on your own.

Apply through your own university. If your college has a special program or relationship with a British or Irish university, your arrangements may be simple and painless. You pay your own college tuition, and advisors in both countries handle most of the paperwork. Credit transfer is easy, and you can maintain your financial aid benefits. If you would like to apply through your own university, visit your study abroad advisor and see if a program exists. While this is how many students get to Ireland and Britain, some find the available destinations limited, or decide that they don't want to study abroad with their own classmates.

Apply through another university. If your college has no study abroad advisor or if the programs it offers don't suit your needs, you can usually apply through another college that offers the programs you want. But be sure to check on credit transfer before you sign on, and be aware that some colleges restrict access to other options to fill their own rosters. The most complete guide to all university programs is *Study in the United Kingdom and Ireland,* published by IIE. It is a useful handbook, listing over eight hundred programs in Britain and Ireland, although it contains only brief, technical information on each one. It is also expensive, so see if you can borrow it from your advisor or the local library. The institute has advisors and libraries at centers in Chicago, Denver, Houston, San Francisco, and at their main office in New York.

Apply directly. Direct application is the least common way to study abroad but the most independent and often the most rewarding. This is not only for the backpack-toting, "I'll buy the toothbrush later" crowd—anyone can try this route. You are admitted to universities as a regular student, take classes with the British or Irish, arrange your own bank accounts, and live in dormitories or flats in town like your Irish and British counterparts. Government financial aid sometimes transfers, and overseas universities generally welcome independent applicants, providing the same advising and support services they do for students in U.S. and Canadian college programs. Tuition was once a lot cheaper overseas, but this is changing, according to several North American students and study abroad advisors, as British universities in particular lose government funding and discover how much overseas students will pay. Still, direct applicants might pay less than those who go through their own university or on another college program.

Direct application requires research and a certain amount of special effort. Some small colleges prohibit it outright, restricting students to their own study abroad programs. Part of the reason is money, and while colleges have a right to expect you to pay four full years of tuition (they have costs and budgets to meet, like everyone else), they won't admit this to you. The official explanation will be a concern for controlling the educational experience, despite the fact that living and studying in a British or Irish university is educational, no matter how you get there. Other universities may make it difficult for you to apply independently by preventing credit transfer or pushing their own study abroad programs without explaining other options. *Remember that many British and Irish universities want qualified students to come and don't care how they get there.* If you apply directly, you not only get a terrific adventure that might allow for greater independence than the official program, you also develop a much more sophisticated understanding of educational exchange.

To apply directly for admission to a British or Irish university for a term, two terms, or a year abroad, do the following:

1. Visit your study abroad advisor and find out if there is a policy on direct application. If it's prohibited, ask the advisor to explain the reasons for the policy, and explain why you wish to study abroad independently. Maybe you can come to some kind of agreement. Ask about taking a semester or a year off. If direct application is allowed, find out if your home university has a recommended procedure.

If you want overseas classes to count toward your major, it's a good idea to speak to your academic or major advisor about your plans for study abroad. The sooner you get a list of possible courses to present to this advisor, the better. As a rule, it's often difficult to get approval for courses in your major, although this depends on your university and advisor. Your department may have special rules or procedures concerning credit transfer, and it's important to learn and follow them. Remember that you don't always get grades for courses taken overseas, often only a "pass" or "fail," so if a class is very important for your major, you might want to take it at home.

2. Write early (see schedule on page 10) to the British/Irish university you'd like to attend to request a catalog *(prospectus)* and an application form. The student union may publish an alternative prospectus which offers student perspectives on such subjects as housing, academics, and social life. The best route is to request both the official and alternative prospectuses for the administration's and student union's points of view. When writing, feel free to raise any specific questions you may have about courses, living arrangements, prerequisites, and other concerns.

3. Apply. The prospectus may include an application form (request it specifically when you first write) which differs from your average form for colleges in North America. For British and Irish students, admission depends largely on the results of *A-level* exams (in England, Wales, and Northern Ireland), *highers* (in Scotland), or *leaving*

certificate exams (in Ireland). Requiring applicants to write long
personal statements is not a tradition in these countries. Keep in mind
that because North Americans are now aggressively courted by universities since they pay higher tuition fees and fill budgets slashed by
government cutbacks, forms tend to be simple. They'll ask for your
age, address, sex, marital status, information on your home university, health data, a transcript, at least one academic reference, and
perhaps a short statement about the reasons for your choice of a
university or polytechnic.

In Britain and Ireland you don't always apply to the university as
such but to a particular department (or *faculty)* within the university
(this should be clear from the application). Once accepted by a
department, you can sometimes take classes in other departments
(the policy varies from institution to institution), but you still belong
to the department that accepts you. One University of London student
found this out the hard way: although he took only arts courses, he was
charged the science fee (science courses often cost more) because he
had been accepted by a science department, not an arts department.
You also choose courses at the time you apply, although placement
is not guaranteed. It's very important at this point to check again with
your academic advisor about the courses you plan to take and to get
preliminary approval for credit transfer *in writing,* not only for
courses in your major but also from all other departments represented
in your choice of courses. Your study abroad advisor may even provide
a special form. Get the full name, title, and address of every advisor and
faculty member who signs this form, so you can write them if your
courses change after arrival overseas.
Application deadlines for British and Irish universities seem late by
U.S. and Canadian standards, *but apply early*—you're more likely to
get university housing. Deadlines vary, but most adhere to the following pattern:

Basic Application Deadlines (JYA)

Autumn term admission:	**April 1**
Spring term admission:	**November 1**
Summer term admission:	**February 1**

You may hear from universities quickly, sometimes within two weeks, although a month or two is more common.

ADDITIONAL OPTIONS—ENGLAND, WALES, AND NORTHERN IRELAND

Full-Degree Programs—Overview

Undergraduate degrees take about three years to complete in England, Wales, and Northern Ireland. Students from these areas once took *O-level* (ordinary level) exams or CSE (Certificate of Secondary Education) exams at age sixteen. These have been replaced by the single GCSE (General Certificate of Secondary Education) exam. All students are expected to remain in school until age sixteen, and to then take the GCSE. After the GCSE, some students move on to *sixth-form colleges,* a unique tier of education falling between high school (secondary education) and college (higher education). At sixth-form colleges, students from England, Wales, and Northern Ireland prepare for the more specialized *A-level* (advanced level) examinations and enter university at around nineteen years of age. The new *AS-level* (advanced supplemental level) exams, which are broader in scope and allow students to focus on a greater variety of subjects, may replace A-levels as the standard university requirement. Not all students follow this traditional route to higher education. As in North America, older, second-career adults (known as *mature students* in Britain and Ireland) and others with unique qualifications are now entering universities in increasing numbers.

Studying for a full degree overseas can give you an advantage in the race for jobs on your return home. British and Irish degrees are often looked upon favorably by U.S. and Canadian employers, although your chances may be better if you've attended an institution with a widely recognized name. Your extensive international experience will be another significant plus. However, four years abroad will leave you out of touch with your home culture and educational system, and your outlook will probably be a lot more British or Irish than North American. This sudden shift in expectations and attitude can leave you struggling with cultural baggage that other Americans won't understand. If you choose to stay in Europe, you'll be better qualified than someone with a North American degree, but work permits can be tricky to obtain. On the other hand, after four years abroad, you may have married a local.

Students from the United States and Canada are generally expected to complete one or two years of work at a North American university before applying for a full-degree program in England, Wales, or Northern Ireland, because freshman year North American college courses are usually considered comparable to A-level (sixth form college level) work. Several Advanced Placement (AP) examination grades are often equally acceptable in meeting requirements for admission. Whatever your qualifications, it never hurts to fill out an application. The only cost to you is the postage.

The Joint Matriculation Board (JMB), run by and for the universities of Manchester, Leeds, Liverpool, Sheffield, and Birmingham, requires North Americans to meet the following requirements:

Requirements for Admission—JMB Universities

For Americans:
- high school transcript of "C" average or better
- SAT scores of at least 500
- either three Achievement tests (one must be in a foreign language, one must be science or math) or two Advanced Placement exams with scores of 3 or better

For Canadians:
- Senior matriculation diploma with passes in English and four other approved subjects
- Achievement of Grade XIII in Ontario, Grade XI or a Secondary V, the *Diploma d'Études Collegiales* (DEC) in Quebec, or Grade XII in all other provinces

---

For more information, contact the JMB directly by writing to the Secretary of the Board, Joint Matriculation Board, Manchester M15 6EU, England; tel. (061) 273-2565.

Full-Degree Programs—How to Apply

Remember that you're probably applying to a particular department for a specific degree program, not to the university as a whole. Certain departments may require additional qualifications for admission. However, once you satisfy the requirements listed above, here's how to apply directly for a full three or four years of study toward an undergraduate degree from a university in England, Wales, or Northern Ireland.

Write to the Universities Central Council on Admissions (or UCCA) at Post Office Box 28, Cheltenham, Glos GL50 3SA, United Kingdom; tel. (0242) 222444. Ask for a copy of their handbook, *How to Apply for Admission to a University,* which includes an application form with instructions and an up-to-date listing of all courses offered by each university.

Apply to the universities you'd like to attend. You can apply to five separate universities on the UCCA form. If you apply to Cambridge, however, you can't apply to Oxford and vice versa, because neither institution can imagine how you'd possibly choose one over the other.

For England, Wales, and Northern Ireland

Deadlines for completing your UCCA application:

October 15   for candidates applying to
                                   Oxford or Cambridge

December 15   for all other universities

After August 26, UCCA operates a *clearing scheme,* where candidates who failed to get into any universities on the basis of their UCCA forms can try again. Four universities can be named in the clearing, and if those universities have vacancies, they may accept you.

Buckingham University is the only private university in the U.K. and is not part of the UCCA scheme. It has a two-year program (eight terms, four terms per year). To obtain more information and/or apply to Buckingham, write to them directly for an application form: Admissions Officer, The University of Buckingham, Buckingham MK18 1EG, England; tel. (0280) 814080.

Polytechnics (England and Wales Only)

Polytechnics are colleges that began in the 1960s and offer some university-type courses but are known more for vocational courses. Until recently, polys awarded students degrees from the Council for National Academic Awards (CNAA), but this is set to change. Over the next few years CNAA will be abolished and the polys will become self-accrediting institutions with their own Royal Charters—in other words, the polys will become universities.

Currently, there are thirty polytechnics in Britain, offering diverse programs and professional training in many fields. They offer courses like catering, photography, film, or design, which aren't available at (most) universities, as well as more traditional liberal arts courses. Despite the changes, there is still a rivalry between universities and polytechnics, with universities claiming a more exalted status and better facilities, but if you compare the variety of course options, polytechnics often have the upper hand. Some people think of the polys as U.S.-style state universities.

Many polytechnics offer JYA programs to North American and other foreign students. To get a list of courses offered, ask for the *First Degree and Diploma of Higher Education Courses* directory from the Council for National Academic Awards, 344-354 Gray's Inn Road, London WC1X 8BP, United Kingdom; tel. (071) 278-4411. However, UCCA will probably take over responsibility for polytechnic application, so contacting them will get you the latest information.

ADDITIONAL OPTIONS—SCOTLAND

Full-Degree Programs—Overview

In Scotland, many undergraduate degrees require four years instead of three for completion. Scottish high school students (only sixteen or seventeen years of age) take *highers*, general examinations in several fields similar to Advanced Placement exams offered in the States. At university, an *ordinary course* is a general degree course lasting three years, while an *honours course* (becoming more popular) takes four years, involving two years of specialized study. What follows are the requirements for North American students interested in pursuing a full-degree program in Scotland:

Requirements for Admission: Scottish Universities

- **SATs & Achievements:** minimum scores of 550 each on SAT verbal and math tests, plus a minimum of 600 on three Achievement tests or

- **SATs & APs:** minimum scores of 550 each on SAT verbal and math, plus a 4 or 5 on two Advanced Placement (AP) examinations or

- **Freshman Year:** successful completion of a freshman year at an accredited U.S. or Canadian university or college (although not a junior college).

Full-Degree Programs—How to Apply

To apply for a full-degree program at a Scottish university, you follow the same procedure outlined for institutions in England, Wales, and Northern Ireland. See page 12 for specific information.

For Scotland

Deadline for completing your UCCA application:

December 15   of the year prior to study

Scottish Central Institutions

The fourteen polytechnic-like higher education establishments in Scotland are known as *central institutions*. The "big five" are Napier College, Dundee College of Technology, the Robert Gordon's Institute of Technology (RGIT), Paisely College of Technology, and Glasgow College. Each central institution must be applied to directly. Contact the British Council (see appendix A for address) for a list of these.

ADDITIONAL OPTIONS—IRELAND

Full-Degree Programs—Overview

In Ireland, students take *intermediate exams* at age sixteen and can leave school at this point if they wish. If they choose to continue their education, the next step up the ladder is the *leaving certificate*, granted after they pass seven *leaving examinations* (subjects must include English, Irish, and math). Leaving exams, held annually in June, are the culmination of five years of study: "everything rides on them, they're weeks of pure hell." Seventeen-year-old Irish students gain either an ordinary pass on their leaving certificate, comparable to the O-levels in England, Wales and Northern Ireland, or an honors higher level pass, closer to the A-levels. After these exams, some go on to university (or third-level education).

North American students require the following for admission:

Requirements for Admission: Irish Universities

For National University of Ireland colleges (including Cork, Galway, Dublin)
- high school transcript
- SAT results
- three Achievement tests

For Trinity College, University of Limerick, and Dublin City University
- one year at an accredited institution in the U.S. or Canada

---

Full-Degree Programs—How to Apply

Again, remember that you're applying to a particular department for a particular degree course, not to the university as a whole. *Irish universities tend to limit students to courses in the department that accepts them.* You can always try to buck the system once you get there, and students report that confidence and perseverance sometimes pay off, but be forewarned.

Once you've satisfied the requirements listed above, you can apply directly for a full three or four years of study toward an undergraduate degree at an Irish university. Write to the Central Applications Office

(CAO) for an application form and instructions at Central Applications Office, Tower House, Eglinton Street, Galway, Republic of Ireland; tel. (091) 63318, 63269.

For Ireland

Deadline for completing your Irish CAO application:

December 15   of the year prior to study
(If your application arrives before January 15, it still may be considered)

Other Irish Central Applications Office (CAO) Study Options

There are two other options for studying in Ireland that you may wish to consider. The National College of Art and Design (NCAD) offers studio arts courses (painting, sculpture, drawing, photography) which are not available at Irish universities. The Dublin Institute for Technology offers five colleges of higher education, two focusing on technology, one on marketing, one on commerce, and one on catering. Write to both institutions directly for information on study abroad: National College of Art and Design, 100 Thomas Street, Dublin 8; tel. (01) 711377; and Dublin Institute for Technology, 14 Upper Mount Street, Dublin 2; tel. (01) 762652.

Irish Regional Technical Colleges

There are eight *regional technical colleges (RTCs)* in the Republic of Ireland, similar to English/Welsh polytechnics and Scottish central institutions, which are more specialized and technical in nature than Irish universities. Their degree courses are generally four years long, and their phone numbers are listed in appendix B. If you're interested in applying, write to them directly.

NOTE: If you're a junior (or, in special cases, a sophomore) and interested in transferring to an Irish or British university, you might consider applying directly as a visiting student (short-term student, JYA) and then transferring after your year abroad. Not all universities allow this, but if it works you avoid the UCCA/CAO process. Realize, however, that no matter how you apply, you probably won't get credit at your university back home for the two years you've completed.

2

The World According to Britain and Ireland

B ritain and Ireland are geographical terms referring to two islands in the northwest corner of Europe. The island of Britain includes the three separate countries of England, Wales, and Scotland, while the island of Ireland includes the Republic of Ireland and the U.K.-administered region of Northern Ireland. The United Kingdom of Great Britain and Northern Ireland (U.K.) is the political union of England, Scotland, and Wales, plus Northern Ireland. The term *Britain* (or Great Britain) is often used loosely to refer to the U.K. as well. *British Isles* refers to both islands, but the Irish, not being British, understandably dislike this term. Actually, some nit-picking British may dispute the term "British" itself: "The only British," they will say, "are the Hong Kong Chinese and residents of Gibraltar, the Falklands, the British Virgin Islands, and other assorted lumps of rock. Perhaps the Queen is British, too." Britain and Ireland are inhabited by the English, the Welsh, the Scots (never Scotch— that's a drink!), and the Irish.

Although England, Wales, and Scotland are linked together in political union, they are all individual countries with long histories, proud traditions, separate languages, and distinct cultures. Never refer to them as "regions" or "states." Never say "It's great to be in England" while hiking Arthur's Seat above Edinburgh's black spires, or gush how "quaint and English" a tiny town appears in Wales. While you'll encounter a lot of what seems only good-natured, spirited pride and boasting, strong nationalist movements do exist in each of these separate countries: the Scottish National party (or SNP) hopes to cut ties to England and join the European Community (EC) on its own, while the *Meibion Glyndwr* (or "Sons of Glendower") have been known to set fire to English-owned holiday homes in Wales! In Northern Ireland, the Irish Republican Army (IRA) makes international headlines for its nationalist aspirations and actions. *Despite this, all are perfectly safe countries, especially for North Americans on a year abroad.*

The Celtic countries, whose languages and cultures derive historically from the Celts, include Wales, Scotland (only in the Western Highlands and islands), Ireland, Cornwall (southwest England), and Brittany (northwest France). Again, while some of these are not politically distinct (or certainly not as distinct as they'd like to be), they think of themselves as separate countries.

THE COMMONWEALTH

The Commonwealth is what is left of Britain's once extensive empire, now a federation of former colonies, trusts, and territories with independent governments and sovereignty of their own. Informally linked to the British Crown, these nations—Canada, New Zealand, and Australia (but, emphatically *not* the independent Republic of Ireland!)—contribute to scholarship funds for education abroad, meet to discuss topics of world interest, and maintain special relationships for information, technology, and work exchange. Americans, for instance, must spend one hundred dollars to get a six-month work permit for Britain, while for a much smaller fee the Commonwealth Canadians next door can work for a longer period with fewer restrictions.

The U.S. is decidedly non-Commonwealth (something to do with tea and taxes), although one student reports that his university application included the instruction "Check this box if you are from the U.S., Canada, or other Commonwealth countries."

If you're in London and interested in learning more about the Commonwealth, visit the Commonwealth Institute on Kensington High Street, with its exhibits on member nations and a gift shop selling interesting and expensive crafts from around the world.

THE EUROPEAN COMMUNITY

Ireland and Britain belong to the European Community, a group of twelve nations planning to form a single economic market in 1992. After this landmark date, borders will open, and any European will be able to work or study in any European country without restriction. Forming this new Europe is a complicated process, and MEPs (Members of the European Parliament) meet in the French city of Strasbourg to discuss Community issues. The Belgian capital of Brussels is the administrative headquarters of the EC. Britain, in particular, has expressed strong concerns over a feared loss of autonomy once it is accepted into this "United States of Europe."

> The EC countries in 1991 are Belgium, Denmark, France, Germany, Great Britain, Greece, Ireland, Italy, Luxembourg, the Netherlands, Portugal (including the Azores, Madeira), and Spain (including the Canary Islands, Balearic Islands).

OTHER "BRITISH" ISLANDS

The Channel Islands. The self-governing Channel Islands near the French coast are subject to British law. The two main islands are Jersey and Guernsey, with tiny Sark, Alderney, and Herm nearby. In 1066, the Norman Duke William the Conqueror invaded England, and some Norman islanders still view Britain as one of their territories. Today, the island's inhabitants are a mixture of Normans and wealthy British who have settled there since World War II. A distinctive Norman-French language still survives in the more remote island villages.

The Isle of Man. A separate island nation off the northwest coast of England, the Isle of Man has its own laws, government, police, and the oldest continuous parliamentary legislature (Tynwald) in the world. The Isle is within easy reach of Britain and Ireland, with strong historical ties to both. Lenient tax laws have attracted hundreds of wealthy British, and the native Manx population is now in decline. The Isle of Man is a Crown dependency, purchased by the British government in 1828 for £417, but it retains considerable independence over customs and tax laws.

The Orkney Islands. The Orkneys are an archipelago of sixty-seven islands off the northern coast of Scotland. Several hundred years ago, the story goes, Denmark ran short of cash and borrowed money from the Scots, who took the islands as security. Apparently Denmark never felt like paying off the eight thousand old Dutch florins to recover the islands. Islanders speak English (a Scots variety), but the Orkneys have strong historical ties to Norway, and the original language, *Norn,* is a mixture of Norwegian and Gaelic.

The Shetland Islands. The Shetlands are another set of islands belonging to Scotland but with strong links to Norway—Norsemen inhabited the Shetlands in the eighth century. "Sir Patrick Spens," a fourteenth-century ballad, tells the story of the daughter of the King of Norway, who drowned on the way to Scotland. Her dowry was the islands, which Scotland claimed despite her death.

The Falkland Islands. The Falkland Islands are referred to as the Islas Malvinas by the Argentines, who still claim these nearby islands as their own. The British went to war to protect this Crown colony in

1982. The British victory boosted Margaret Thatcher into further years of power because of the patriotic fervor she and the war stirred up (despite the fact that the main inhabitants of the islands were, and continue to be, sheep).

Sealand. A World War II antiaircraft tower off the Essex (southeast England) coastline and abandoned after the war, Sealand was claimed by Roy and Joan Bates, the self-styled Prince and Princess of Sealand. The concrete complex issues its own money, coins, stamps, and even passports. They were approached by the Argentines during the Falklands War, but the Bates remained loyal to, if independent from, the United Kingdom.

THE WEATHER

The weather in Britain and Ireland is rumored to be dark, wet, and nasty...and guess what? The rumors are true, but only partially. The extent of darkness, wetness, and nastiness varies greatly across the two islands, and weeks of bright sunshine are common in both the summer and early fall. In general the further north and west you go, the darker, wetter, and nastier the weather becomes, while the southeastern parts of Britain can be dry and sunny. The key weather word for both Britain and Ireland is *changeable.*

Ireland and Britain have generally mild climates; don't expect DC-style heat waves or Minnesota snows. The mercury usually stays within a comfortable, above-freezing range. In spring, summer, and autumn the temperatures are reasonable (although in the north of Scotland, it'll probably feel cool). Winter temperatures only seem cold when you're living in dormitories without central heating in a country that's often wet.

The biggest weather problem, especially for students in the north, is the lack of light in winter—you might see the sun in Aberdeen from 9:00 A.M. til 3:30 P.M. only. "It gets you depressed," says an American at Dundee. "I felt pretty miserable through February and March." "If you get here in January," she warns, "the weather is the pits." This does have a good side: in late spring and early summer, it stays light past 10:00 P.M.!

The watchword is: be prepared. Don't expect Britain or Ireland to be the sunniest or driest year of your life; umbrellas, sweaters, and waterproof coats are a must (buy them overseas). But don't always blame irritability or depression on the weather—homesickness or culture shock also dampen one's spirits. And you might be surprised; the greenhouse effect may warm these islands up, and their rainy reputation may change.

OVERVIEW: ENGLAND, WALES, SCOTLAND, IRELAND

Before heading overseas to Britain or Ireland, it helps to understand a little about the countries you'll be studying and traveling in. While this book is in no way a comprehensive reference, it will give you a general idea of the history and social structure of each country.

England

Although not large, England is an incredibly diverse land of rivalries and divisions originating from centuries past. A series of invaders, from Celts to Romans to Normans, helped established the patchwork nature of the country, which survives in language, culture, and regionalism to this day.

England once lay blanketed under thick forests, which were felled rapidly after the arrival of agricultural peoples from Belgium and France over 4,000 years ago. The modern-day grassy, rolling, hilly downland of southern England is largely their work, along with mysterious Stonehenge and the path-marking cairns, piles of stones placed along well-traveled footpaths throughout the land. The Celts, who arrived around 650 B.C., continued the tradition of immigration to England, bringing further advances in agriculture, commerce, and a new religion with them across the Channel.

The Romans followed the Celts around 55 B.C., establishing the first road system, the famous baths at Bath, and many market communities like St. Albans, Colchester, and—at the time—tiny London. During their rule, Christianity spread and supplanted older Celtic traditions. The Romans also built Hadrian's Wall, a seventy-four mile barrier to the Celtic tribes of Scotland, and ruled over most of England and Wales for nearly four hundred years.

The next invasion involved the Angles and Saxons from northwestern Germany, who established a system of laws and laid the foundation for the class divisions that are still in place today. They ruled until 1066, when William the Conqueror defeated the Saxon King, Harold II, at the Battle of Hastings, inaugurating centuries of Norman-Viking rule. Under Norman influence, the hierarchical system left by the

Anglo-Saxons was refined, and the aristocracy established throughout the land.

One firmly entrenched aristocracy still resides in southeast England, with London as its center and the prosperous Home Counties (which include Surrey and Kent) surrounding. London has long been the nation's financial center (currently concentrated in the original Roman area known as "The City"), and years of speculative misadventures have fueled the resentment of other regions (especially the north) toward the conservative southeast.

The West Country, the pointed finger of England that reaches from Stonehenge in Wiltshire to the Celtic tip of Cornwall (one of the last regions conquered by the Anglo-Saxons), is a popular tourist area for the legions who flood in from the southeast each year to rent cottages by the wild shores and drink strong, potent scrumpy-cider in picturesque seaside pubs.

The Midlands is a spacious, varied area dotted with farms, cathedrals, and coal-burning plants, that stretches across the country's midsection. The Midlands are comparable to the American Midwest, with industrial cities amidst areas of low, rolling croplands. The home of Robin Hood, Nottinghamshire is probably the most famous area, although don't expect to see much of the legendary Sherwood Forest, which has been largely cut down. The shire is, however, the recognized home of the world's first garden gnome.

The North of England is known throughout the country for friendliness and good beer, especially when the region is contrasted with its rival, the southeast. Only the fifteenth-century War of the Roses between the royal houses of York and Lancaster has provoked greater enmity within the region than with the rich counties surrounding London. Once considered an economic basket case after the collapse of much of the mining industry, the North has done well for itself in recent years, while the southeast has suffered. The North is home to the Yorkshire moors, a wet, heathered landscape suffused with legends of Dracula and werewolves (the classic "American Werewolf in London" was filmed here), and the Dales, a nearby area of greener hills.

Wales

Wales is a distinct country, with a Celtic heritage shared with Ireland, Cornwall, the Highlands and islands of Scotland, and Brittany in northwest France. The Celts were a fierce and lyric people, and they fought successively with the Romans, the Goidelic Celts from Ireland, and most recently the Anglo-Saxons from England. Welsh culture thrives in the green, rolling valleys of the south (the inspiration for *Pobl y Cwm*, "People of the Valleys," a popular Welsh soap opera), and the spectacular northern mountains of the Snowdonia National Park. The National Eisteddfod, a week-long festival celebrating the Welsh traditions of storytelling and song, is held alternately in the north and south of the country each August.

North American students feel thoroughly welcome in Wales and find the Welsh open and hospitable. Many Americans have family links to Wales, and any ties to England are readily forgiven. "The Welsh are easier to make friends with than the English," says an American at Swansea. "They're not as used to Americans. I think that the English, especially Londoners, are pretty jaded." A Canadian at Aberystwyth disagrees: "The English are incredibly friendly because, at least here in the west, they're foreigners, too." "I've learned so much, especially about Wales as a separate nation," says an American at Bangor. "It has helped to be in a culturally unique area, and not a big city like London that's so international."

The most distinctive feature of Wales is the language, far more than the tourist-inspired *lovespoons* (carved wooden spoons signifying friendship and love) hawked by craft shops throughout the country. Although Welsh is spoken by only 20 percent of the population, official signs and University of Wales student union publications and notices are printed in both English and Welsh. Each child has a choice of English or Welsh secondary schools, where classes and even soccer games on the playground are conducted in the chosen language. "Learn some Welsh, at least things like 'thank you' *(diolch yn fawr)*," urges one American at Bangor. "If you try to speak the language, you'll make people smile." You'll hear more Welsh up north, where the culture and language are proudly retained. In the circle of mountains known as the *Snowdonia Ring,* the inhabitants were never conquered; they hid in the hills when the English invaded. Their radical descendants are the Meibion Glyndwr (the Welsh national hero, Owain Glyndwr, briefly booted the English out of Wales in 1401).

As in England, there's a much joked about north/south division. The beautiful rise and fall of the southern valleys are home to *hwntws* ("down below"), the southerners, whom the *gogs* (northerners) describe as "miners who sing in choruses and live by slag heaps." Southerners describe themselves as "much closer, warmer, and friendlier" than gogs, who "speak through their noses and herd sheep." The South is more connected to England than the North, with the M4 motorway and the Severn Bridge inextricably linking the two. Cardiff, the southern capital of Wales, makes an effort to be Welsh, with the National Museum and a few Welsh-only pubs, but it is largely English, and Swansea, with a distinctively seesaw spoken English, doesn't make much of an effort at all. However, Aberystwyth, site of the National Library, is strongly Welsh, boasting a large membership in the nationalist group Plaid Cymru (which wants more autonomy for Wales within a united Europe), and many residents of Bangor, by the mountains of Snowdonia, want total autonomy.

The rivalry with the English is generally light-hearted, although anger at cultural assimilation and economic domination is real enough. A popular bumper sticker reads "If Wales were flat, it would be bigger than England," or as Welsh residents put it, "Can you imagine looking in an encyclopedia for information on your own country, and finding 'see England' under the entry?" Some Welsh place Queen's-head stamps upside-down on letters to protest.

The historical English ownership of Welsh mines and exploitation of Welsh workers are still resented. One prospective Welsh freshman at Aberystwyth claims that "we have a better attitude toward education because we're forced to. We've traditionally pushed children into college as an escape from the mines." "We've been dependent for too long on a few industries controlled by wealthy English owners in London," adds another. "We're a bit jealous of Scotland," notes a third. "A lot of Scottish National party members come to Wales. The Scots are all right; they've managed to keep themselves out from under English control."

The Union Jack, or British flag, is a source of annoyance for some Welsh: "There's a red St. George's Cross for England, a diagonal red on white background St. Patrick's Cross for Ireland, and a white diagonal on blue background St. Andrew's Cross for Scotland, but no St. David's Cross for Wales." "Wales is a principality owned by the Prince of Wales (currently Prince Charles)," offers an English politics student, who's technically right but almost loses his head. Mention Prince Charles and you'll get an earful: "The bastard son of the Queen of England," "He's English, not Welsh," and "It might help if he spoke our language." Not all Welsh feel this way, and many decry the negative effect of this attitude on relations with the English. "I think that separatism and nationalism just cause bad feelings. What good is being moody and exclusive, even if some English are arrogant and look down on the Welsh?" Still, most wryly admit that "if Prince Charles had a royal residence in Wales, we'd probably burn it down."

Several Welsh university colleges—especially Lampeter (St. David's), Aberystwyth, and Bangor—are quite isolated. It can take up to six hours to reach Lampeter from London with a carefully orchestrated ensemble of tube, train, and bus transfers. Unlike many other, more accessible universities, students stick around the campus on weekends, and the social life, parties, pubs, sports, club activities, and union bar remain packed and active. It also means that it's harder for North Americans to flit off to Paris for the weekend, so they tend to make closer friends and learn more about the surrounding area than someone Eurailing half their time away from Surrey or Essex.

Scotland

The Scots (or Scottish) have always been an independent lot, and not even the Romans could subdue them, preferring instead to erect the massive Hadrian's Wall to keep them out. While the country united with England in 1707 and a single Parliament was created, Scotland nevertheless managed to preserve its distinct legal and educational systems to the present day.

Scotland is reputed to have as many divisions and rivalries as its neighbor to the south. Edinburgh, you'll hear, is filled with the impolite, snobby attitudes of London and is home to many who've moved up from the south of England. "They're tied up in their own business, push past you in the street, and wouldn't think of holding open a door!" Glasgow, in contrast, is described as a "laid-back, diverse city with a reputation for roughness and drunkenness, but people have a great sense of humor and will give you the time of day." Both friends and complete strangers will call you Jimmy, even if your name is Hildegard or Mel. "It really stuck in Edinburgh's craw that Glasgow, which boasts the National Opera and Symphony, won European City of Culture for 1990," say many Glaswegians, while residents of picture-perfect Edinburgh scoff that "all Glasgow did to celebrate was keep the bars open late." Glaswegians who go to St. Andrews, considered even more upper class and English than Edinburgh University, are said to change. "They get very public [private] school and lose their accent; it's frightening really." Dundee is a small city, centrally located in an area of the Tay Estuary, which is dotted with castles. In the far north, Aberdeen, the oil capital of Europe, is a regular winner of the "Britain in Bloom" contest.

Many English students attend Scottish universities, especially the ancient St. Andrews, Glasgow, Aberdeen, and Edinburgh, which have acquired a strong snob appeal for *yahs* (public school types from the south dying to study art history up north). At these four institutions, English students outnumber or equal the number of Scots. This provokes controversy, especially among supporters of the Scottish National party (SNP) who call for devolution, or secession, from the United Kingdom. "Scotland's very much a separate country already, with its own legal and educational systems," explains an SNP member. "There's really just a treaty with England to keep us in." According to many Scots, "English students mix in perfectly well if they're from the North, but southerners can act like they're superior, especially the yahs. They throw these 'cocktail parties,' and try to act grown-up but just appear stupid. The worst are rich overseas students who attended English public schools."

Because of Scotland's geographical position and historical links with Norway (the Vikings invaded several northern Scottish islands preceding William the Conquerer's arrival in 1066), there are many Scandinavians at Scottish universities, especially Norwegians. They are particularly conspicuous when they annually (and drunkenly) celebrate Norwegian Constitution Day on May 17.

Dancing has a proud history in Scotland, and clubs, halls, and even academic faculties hold *céilidhs* (pronounced 'kaylees'), traditional dancing like North American square dancing. Country dances are also popular but more complicated than céilidhs, while highland dancing is solo Scottish dancing that originated in the Highlands and Western Islands. The *Gaelic Mod* is a Highland/island choral group competition held in October in a different part of the country each year. Men do wear kilts in Scotland for formal events; you rent a kilt as you would rent a tux back home.

If you're in Scotland in January, you'll definitely encounter Burns Night, the celebration of the birth of the great Scottish poet Robert Burns on the 25th of January. You'll eat *haggis* (the national dish consisting of sheep guts in sheep stomach, slathered in tart brown sauce), *tatties* (potatoes), and *neeps* (turnips). A kilted man wanders around the dining hall playing bagpipes, while another follows him with the plate of haggis, reciting Burns's poem, "To a Haggis," while slicing off portions. Not to be missed.

Around Christmas and New Year's, try to catch a pantomime— a fun, campy version of a well-known fairy tale performed at local theaters. This is a Scottish tradition requiring heavy audience participation. You boo and hiss when the easily identified bad guy appears on stage and laugh when the obviously made-up panto-mime dame (a man dressed up as a woman) cries out in mock distress. You might also attempt a game of *shinty,* considered by highlanders to be their national sport; it's a fun and semidangerous Irish/Scots form of hockey, where the ball is permitted to travel above your waist.

Ireland

The land of leprechauns, Guinness, St. Patrick and other good Catholics, Ireland (or Eire) is a country rich in history and legend. Originally inhabited by superstitious and warring tribes of Celts, Ireland was divided into four separate kingdoms: Leinster, Ulster, Munster, and Connaught. Following the Roman conquest of England, Catholic missionaries did their job so well that it's still tough to find a condom almost two thousand years later. The Romans were followed by the Anglo-Saxon English, who attempted to rule the country for various periods. The Great Famine of 1845-49 devastated the popula-tion, and thousands fled to North America. Every Irish student knows about the Easter Uprising of 1916, which began five years of bloody fighting that routed the English army from Dublin but firmly en-trenched it in Belfast.

Although a small island, Ireland varies greatly across its wet, green expanse. Dublin, the capital, is considered the New York of the country, the cultural and entertainment center with the high-est level of crime, while the rest of the nation basks in virtue and values and hangs on to its Celtic roots (several areas remain Irish-speaking). There's no denying the natural beauty, mystery, and tradition of the southern and western regions that gave rise to legends of tiny green men. Yet Dublin boasts more theaters, cin-emas, and bookstores than the country towns, so while the streets are safer in Cork and Galway, you can feel a little isolated or cut off. Dublin is within the Pale, which is the Anglo-Irish area of Ireland that has strong historical ties to England, while the other regions of Ulster, Munster, and Connaught are beyond the Pale, or more strongly Celtic.

In the North of the country, the dispute over the six counties of Ulster has festered for the past four hundred years. In a short guide-book it is impossible to explain all the various ins and outs of "The Troubles," as the situation is euphemistically described by politicians and journalists, but take the following advice: go ahead and ask questions, but don't voice uninformed opinions, and listen carefully to what people have to say.

Many North American students choose Ireland because of family connections: "My last name is Murphy." "My grandparents are from Ballyshannon." "I'm from Boston, so where did you expect me to go?" The Irish are accustomed to meeting students interested in their family roots, and most are happy to help you find them. Americans in particular often encounter a comparable level of interest in stories about the United States, where many young Irish head each year to work, legally and illegally.

St. Patrick's Day (March 17) is not the day of green ice cream, green public fountains, green McDonald's shakes, and green beer hysteria popular on the American East Coast, but more a day to take off work and go to church. There are small parades in most cities, but the largest in Dublin is mainly for tourists from Boston and Chicago. Think of it as Thanksgiving in the States. If you're with your relatives or friends' families, it's good food and conversation; if not, it can be a rather lonely holiday (although the pubs do open in the evenings and most Irish would love to hear your stories about all the green back home).

For many, pub life is a major part of studying abroad in Ireland. Club activities (sports included) often finish meets or gatherings with pints of strong Irish beer at the "local." Many Irish pubs offer live music sessions, performances of traditional Irish music and song, where the guitar, harp, and flute predominate.

Irish students and others pepper their everyday language with colorful expressions and foul words. This is not a country where euphemisms like "gosh" and "comfort station" go down well. If someone thanks you for the "great crack" at your party, don't panic. *Crack* to the Irish is merely a good time, or gossip. "What's the crack?" is simply "What's up?" or "What's happening?"

NOTE: Irish newspapers are generally more expensive than British ones because they're subject to a publications tax. They're sold without tax only in student union shops.

3

Before Leaving and upon Arrival

BEFORE LEAVING

Packing

Americans are notorious for bringing U-Hauls full of clothes, a year's supply of aspirin, vitamin pills, toothpaste, and other extraneous items when they travel to Britain and Ireland. One student had to have her down comforter and flannel sheets. The important thing to remember when packing for study abroad is to *pack light*. Sure you're going for six months or a year, but practically everything available in your home country is also available in Ireland and Britain. In addition, luggage limits on most airlines are strictly enforced; you'll pay for all the extra boxes and duffel bags. The less you take, the less encumbered you are, and the more freedom you have to travel and move around. Plus your friends and family won't hate you as they struggle through the airport with your bags. Before you compile your packing list, check first to see what items will be provided by the university; for example, many dormitories provide pillows, linens, and blankets at no extra charge.

The greatest type of luggage ever invented is the backpack, which holds a ton of clothing and other items yet feels comfortable and leaves your hands free. It also serves as gear for when you head off hosteling, hitching, or Eurailing during your year abroad. An internal frame pack is superior to an external frame pack because the support system is cushioned and hidden inside the fabric of the pack, not exposed where it can get caught on people's coats or whack fellow travelers in the face. Get a pack with a hip belt that shifts the weight from shoulders to hips. Some packs convert into suitcases as well. A small day pack will help when making short trips away from the university. Duffel bags also make excellent luggage—they're soft and malleable, and they fit under seats and carry a lot.

Britain and Ireland can be cold and damp, so sweaters and good rain gear are essential. Wool sweaters, which stay warm even when wet, are widely available overseas, so unless you're arriving in January, leave most of your own collection home. Sweaters also take up space in your pack, so choose carefully. Eastern Mountain Sports, L.L. Bean, REI, and a host of other outdoors shops sell terrific waterproof shells (raincoats) that can be stuffed in small sacks. To protect yourself from the chill of underheated hostels or university dorms without central heating, bring long underwear, or at least the top portion. A sleeping bag is essential—get one that zips open so it can function as a comforter. Gloves, a scarf, and a rain shield for your pack complete the list of rain- and cold-proof items.

Black clothing was once the standard uniform of British and Irish university students, and still is among some campus cliques. With the growing influence of hip-hop and house music, day-glo colors are more widely worn. Of course, blue jeans, hi-top sneakers, and colorful shirts (especially with the name of a U.S. or Canadian college emblazoned across the front) will immediately identify you as a North American. Nevertheless, blue jeans—black or blue—are tough, durable, and comfortable, and make good sense. They're more expensive in Europe than they are back home, so bring some along.

Footwear is important and shoes and sneakers are expensive, so bring a good pair from home. If you plan to hike (and terrific opportunities exist along long-distance footpaths), bring hiking boots or the smaller and lighter hiking sneakers. These sneakers have thick rubber soles and need less breaking in than boots, but they don't offer the same ankle support.

Other useful suggestions include a Swiss army knife (make sure you pack this in your checked baggage; don't carry a knife on the plane) and a compass, if you plan to do any trail walking. An extra pair of glasses or contact lenses and a copy of your prescription are essential. If you absolutely must bring an electric razor or hair dryer from home, a converter and adapter are both necessary. The converter drops the voltage from the European 220V to the American 110V, while the adapter changes a two-pronged to a three-pronged plug to fit British sockets. There is more than one kind of socket in Britain and Ireland; when the British or Irish buy an appliance, they purchase the appropriate plug separately. Walkmans with tape players provide a lightweight alternative to bulkier stereos; small, inexpensive speakers can be purchased upon arrival and attached through the headphone jack.

Bring small gifts from home: lightweight souvenirs (Mt. St. Helen's ash, anything from Disney, Gateway Arch key chains, etc.), stamps, guidebooks, postcards, coins, refrigerator magnets, baseball caps, American music memorabilia, T-shirts. You'll want a variety of gifts to hand out in exchange for the large and small kindnesses you're sure to receive abroad.

NOTE: Don't bring a razor from home. The Irish and British use a different system and their replacement blades won't fit. Disposables, of course, are fine, but you can get these in Britain and Ireland too.

Important Documents

The following should be carried in a safe place away from your backpack, duffel, or other luggage. You'll be asked to produce some of them for customs, so make sure they are easily accessible when you initially enter the country. The best way to carry documents is in a money belt or neck pouch, to be worn out of sight beneath your clothes.

☞ **Passport.** U.S. passports are valid for ten years, cost around $50, and are available from any passport agency as well as some post offices and courthouses. To get a passport bring proof of citizenship (e.g., birth certificate, immigration papers), two photos, and a photo ID (state ID card or driver's license). It takes two to four weeks to get a passport, but under special circumstances an order can be rushed. To locate the closest passport office, contact the Bureau of Consular Affairs, Office of Passport Services, Department of State, Washington, DC 20520; tel. (202) 647-0518.

Canadian passport applications also require proof of citizenship, two photographs, plus a signature from a professional who has known you for at least two years. They cost C$25 and are available from any passport office. Contact the main office for the one nearest you: Passport Office, Department of External Affairs, Ottawa, Ontario K1A 0G3; tel. (800) 567-9615.

☞ **Visas.** Citizens of the U.S., Canada, Australia, and New Zealand can enter Britain and Ireland without a visa. You're usually permitted to enter Britain for six months, Ireland for three. For longer periods you need to explain the reason for your stay to the immigration officer. When you apply, make sure you request ample time. You might want to travel in Europe before going home, leaving bags and suitcases in Britain or Ireland. Returning (especially to Britain) to pick these up after your immigration stamp expires can mean extra hassles at the ferry terminal or airport. If you anticipate traveling to a non-European country, check with your embassy before you leave home to ensure that you'll have the required documents for entry.

☞ **Letter of acceptance.** The British or Irish university that accepted you will send proof of admission, and the immigration officer will want to see it. The officer will then stamp your passport for the length of time you'll be in the country for study.

☞ **Evidence that you have enough money to support yourself and pay for your course.** If your family is covering the cost of your overseas education, a letter from a parent promising financial support will suffice. Otherwise, bank statements or financial aid forms are required.

☞ **Money.** Bring at least two hundred dollars in local currency (traveler's checks, even in pounds, aren't widely accepted as cash) to reach your campus, buy a few meals, and have a sense of financial security until you set up a bank account. For more information on banking and money, see chapter 7.

☞ **Health insurance.** It's imperative that you have personal health insurance if you're going to be enrolled in a British university for less than six months and in an Irish university for any length of time. If you're in Britain for less than six months, you won't be covered by the National Health Service (NHS), and Ireland has no national insurance. It's a good idea, however, to have personal insurance even though you'll receive NHS coverage in Britain if your course of study lasts longer than six months. Make sure that your U.S. policy covers foreign accidents and illnesses, and bring proof of coverage, including company name and policy number. You may wish to check with Blue Cross/Blue Shield about transferring to Voluntary Health Insurance (VI II) for a year. See chapter 8 for details.

☞ **Student cards.** As a university student you're entitled to discounts on museum entrance, theater tickets, flights, ferries, and an assortment of random items and services across Britain and Ireland. To get special treatment, however, you have to prove that you're a student, not just a young person with a book bag. A number of cards are available to help convince the many officials who'll ask to see your ID (or *matric card* in Scotland).

The International Student Identity Card (or ISIC) is the most common and well recognized student card in the world. The card and discounts were introduced after World War II to help students travel, form international friendships, and develop a better understanding of the postwar world. In addition to discounts, the ISIC provides medical insurance, plus a hundred dollars per day for up to sixty days if you're stuck in a hospital. The ISIC card is sold by the Council on International Educational Exchange. The card is available in Britain for less money, although the British version does not include medical insurance. Bring a passport photo and proof of student status (transcript or current ID) to any Council Travel office, or most budget travel shops in Britain. Rival cards exist, including the International Student Exchange (ISE) card, from International Student Exchange Flights. This card is comparable to ISIC in price and offers medical insurance, but it is not available overseas. If the truth be told, any card, including your own college ID from home, should get you (aside from flights and ferries) most discounts available for students. Contact these organizations for more information: Council on International Educational Exchange, 205 East 42nd Street, New York, NY 10017; tel. (212) 661-1414; International Student Exchange Flights, Post Office Box 22169, Phoenix, AZ 85254; tel. (602) 951-2157.

☞ **Hostel cards.** The cheapest way to stay overnight aside from hauling a tent is in hostels, and there are over four hundred of these dormitory-style housing options in Britain and Ireland. Hostels belong to the International Youth Hostel Federation (IYHF), and a special ID card is often required. The ID can be purchased in the States, where it costs around $20, or in Britain or Ireland, where the price is around £8 if you're over twenty-one and only £4 if you're younger. Accommodation costs are about £4-£7 per night (£1 equals approximately $2). If you don't have a card, you can buy a day membership at individual hostels, but if you'll be traveling a lot, the ID card is worth getting. See appendix E for addresses.

☞ **BUNAC/USIT work permits.** It is possible to work while studying abroad, *although don't expect your earnings to cover living costs or tuition.* The Council on International Educational Exchange issues work permits for a hundred dollars to U.S. citizens over eighteen who are full-time students at an accredited university or college. The British Universities North America Club (BUNAC) permit (or blue card) is valid for six months in Britain, while the Union of Students in Ireland Travel (USIT) permit is valid for four months in the Republic of Ireland. Many students work at pubs (which may also provide room and board), at restaurants, or as office secretaries. The BUNAC permit must be bought before you head overseas, while the USIT permit can usually be issued directly by USIT in Dublin after you land a job. For more information, contact BUNAC, c/o CIEE, 205 East 42nd Street, New York, NY, 10017; tel. (212) 661-1414; or USIT, 19-21 Aston Quay, Dublin 2, Republic of Ireland; tel. (01) 778112, 778117.

☞ **International Driver's License.** Your own driver's license is accepted in Britain and Ireland for up to twelve months, so an International Driver's License is not essential. If you plan to drive in Continental Europe, however, it may prove useful. If you'd like to buy one, contact the AAA before heading abroad.

If you acquire a moped or motorcycle while overseas, you will probably want to join the Automobile Association in Britain or Ireland, which operates similarly to AAA in North America. You can contact them at the following addresses: Basingstoke, Hampshire RG21 2EA, England; tel. (0256) 20123; 23 Rock Hill, Blackrock, Dublin 4, Republic of Ireland; tel. (01) 83355.

☞ **Eurail pass.** The Eurail pass is valid for one or two months of unlimited train travel through Europe. You may want to wait and purchase the cheaper and more extensive Inter Rail card after you arrive overseas (see "Trains" in chapter 6 for the advantages and disadvantages of each).

☞ **Prescriptions.** If you're taking any prescription drugs, make sure the bottles are clearly marked and bring copies of your prescriptions. As mentioned earlier, a copy of the prescription for your glasses or contact lenses is important also.

☞ **List of important numbers.** Write down your passport number, (or better yet, photocopy the first pages of your passport), health insurance policy number, and credit card numbers on a piece of paper in case of loss or theft, and pack it with your valuables separately from your passport.

☞ **Photographs.** You'll need passport-size photographs for a variety of purposes, but wait until you arrive overseas to take pictures if you don't need them before you leave. Photo machines are more common and generally cheaper in Britain and Ireland than they are in North America.

HOUSING

Few universities provide accommodation to students for their full three or four years of study. In Ireland only Trinity College Dublin (TCD), University College Dublin (UCD), University College Galway (UCG), and the University of Limerick have dormitory rooms available. North Americans on a junior year abroad are usually guaranteed housing in Britain, as long as they apply early enough. In Ireland you may have to go apartment hunting (see "Finding Your Own Flat or Bedsit" below).

Self-Catering versus Traditional

There are two main types of university housing, traditional and self-catering. *Traditional halls* are dormitories with a communal dining room where residents eat one or two meals per day. *Self-catering halls* are dormitories with kitchens, organized by floor or by hallway. *Self-catering flats* are student apartments. If you get a choice, pick a self-catering hall or flat. The food in traditional halls is appalling.

North Americans report occasional disappointment with the quality of Irish and British university accommodations, which is surprising considering the state of many U.S. and Canadian college dorms. However, before passing judgment, you need to understand that the British and Irish are generally much less materialistic or obsessed with creature comforts than North Americans are. Keep the following four historically determined points in mind:

1. Britain is crowded, with fifty-five million people and a land mass fifty times smaller than the United States; therefore, the British see housing in a different light. A house unconnected to its neighbor is called a *detached* house—it's something special. Most British and Irish live in *terraced* houses—row homes sharing walls on both sides, or in *semi-detached* houses—pairs of homes sharing a wall. Ireland, with only four million people, is less crowded than England, and parts of Scotland and Wales are luxuriously underpopulated. But don't expect spacious apartments or oceans of dorm room space. It's probably going to be cramped.

2. Central heating is considered a luxury. Whether you're housed in a cinder-block, jerry-built 1960s tower or a charming, fifteenth-century former stable made from locally quarried stone, you'll have to deal with chills and drafts. You may get a flat that heats for only a few hours in the evening or a heater that demands a steady diet of 50p coins. You're expected to keep moving or wear bulky sweaters to keep warm. It gets *cold*, so bring a sleeping bag, invest in blankets, and buy long underwear. The British and Irish use wonderfully thick covered comforters known as *duvets* to keep warm; these may be provided in your dormitory. Expect the strong smell of coal fires in winter, especially in small towns, which often disappear at dusk under clouds of pungent smoke.

3. Plumbing in Britain and Ireland is spartan. Sinks in many dorm rooms are a nice touch, but you'll almost never find a single adjustable faucet (or *tap),* always two, one for hot water and one for cold. Old plumbing and the British/Irish preference for taking fewer baths mean lousy showers. Homes and dormitories may lack showers altogether, and those you do find might suffer from low pressure. If there's no shower head, you hook up a rubber tubing attachment to the taps and sit down in the tub, shaking low-pressure dribbles over your head while praying that a tube won't drop off and send freezing cold or scalding hot water sluicing in your direction.

4. Many British/Irish universities were built in the 1960s, so your university back home may be more architecturally impressive. Aside from Oxford, Cambridge, Trinity College Dublin, Durham, Cork, St. Andrews, and a few Victorian redbricks, many new universities are a harsh blocky jumble of concrete and glass. Students often describe their halls of residence as "modeled after a Swedish prison." Yet don't judge your campus or dormitory by appearance alone: modern architectural harshness is often balanced by modern convenience (heated rooms, functional showers, etc.).

Finding Your Own Flat or Bedsit

Finding your own housing is of special concern for students in Ireland, where little in the way of campus accommodations exists, and for students who applied too late to get university housing. A *flat* is an apartment, and a *bedsit*, which is generally cheaper, is a room in someone's home. *You cannot find a flat from North America.* The landlord will want to meet you and you'll want to view the property, so arrive a few weeks early to start searching before all the other overseas students arrive. It won't be easy; local students will have already nabbed the best spots. Here are some good sources of information:

1. The *University Accommodation Office* usually publishes or posts listings of flats and bedsits. Write them before leaving home for information on finding housing in the area. Also inquire about homestays, local families who may be willing to host overseas students. If you arrive at your university homeless and unprepared, the office may be able to provide you with a listing of local hostels and/or bed and breakfasts (b and bs) to tide you over until you find a place.

2. The *Student Union Welfare Officer* may have a housing list, or the office may have a noticeboard for advertised apartments. Also check with the welfare officer at any of the local polytechnics or art colleges.

3. *Local newspapers,* as in North America, carry advertisements for privately rented flats. Check the evening papers and phone immediately; these flats go fast. Some classified ad abbreviations that you might not recognize include *pw* (for "per week," as most flats are rented on a weekly basis) and *pTV* (for "piped television," or cable TV). This is not the cable you're used to—just the few standard channels brought to your television by an electrical wire. See chapter 11 for information on television licenses.

4. *Shop windows* often have listings for local flats on index cards. Check stationery stores in neighborhoods you'd like to live in.

5. *Estate agents* manage properties for landlords, and are listed in the Yellow Pages. Ask if they'll charge you, and for what (usually drafting the contract). They're not allowed to charge for giving out a list of addresses (although they may try).

6. *Accommodations agencies* check the newspaper listings for you—for a price (usually one week's rent, but there are horror stories about higher fees). It's usually best to do the legwork yourself.

7. *Pubs* occasionally rent rooms to students, especially in Ireland (in England and particularly London, most of these rooms are for live-in staff).

Once you get a contact, set up an appointment for viewing the flat. Use the same criteria as you would in the U.S., and don't be afraid to ask questions. Try the faucets, flush the toilets, make sure the locks (including the locks on windows) are secure, check the stove and the refrigerator. Be sure to find out how the heat works and if it is adequate, and ask how to turn on the hot water. Ask about utilities and other fees, and make sure you inquire about any retainers or deposits that may be charged to hold the flat over vacations. Finally, inquire if you will be responsible for repairs to the flat.

Your *tenancy agreement* (or contract) should include the amount of rent and deposit, the dates when the rent is due, the duration of the tenancy, the repairs for which the landlord is responsible, the services the landlord will provide, the landlord's right of entry, which of the rates (utilities), if any, the landlord will pay, rules regarding subletting the flat, and the period of notice to terminate the contract. *Remember to get everything in writing.*

Then, before moving in, check that the gas, electricity, and phone bills have been paid by the landlord or previous tenants in full up to the date you move in. Contact the appropriate offices to get the bills in your name and arrange for the meters to be read on the day you move in. If anything is broken or damaged, report it to the landlord immediately, in writing.

When you buy a hair dryer, fan, or other electric appliance in Britain or Ireland, it comes without a plug! You're expected to purchase and attach the bulky plastic contraption yourself, connecting all the appropriate wires without electrocuting yourself with the European, life-threatening 220-240 volts. These wires are color-coded as follows:

New System		Old System (not common)	
Brown:	LIVE	Red:	LIVE
Blue:	neutral	Black:	neutral
Green and Yellow:	ground	Green:	ground

There's usually a simple wiring diagram packed with new plugs, and your Swiss army knife will come in handy. *Remember: when plugging anything in (especially if you've wired the plug yourself), make sure the tiny switch on the socket is turned off. Turn it on only after you've firmly inserted the plug.*

Once you've moved into your new home, if you have an emergency repair problem, the landlord is required (by law) to fix it within twenty-one days. "Damage to the structure, exterior, and installations of the flat" constitutes the legal definition of an *emergency* and includes the roof, walls, floor, windows, plumbing (baths, toilets, sinks), electrical wiring, gas piping, fixed heaters, and water heaters.

Don't protest late repairs by withholding your rent—this breaks the terms of your contract. If nothing happens within twenty-one days, contact your university accommodations office or the union welfare officer for advice.

Americans-Only Dormitories

As with all-American courses where overseas students are grouped together, some universities are finding it convenient to group overseas students in special housing. This is a lousy idea because it isolates North Americans and causes them to "clique up." Avoid these dorms and live with the British or Irish.

Conference Centers

Because of British government cutbacks to education and the need to seek outside funding, some universities are usurping student housing for higher-paying customers. Businesses, corporations, and trade associations pay more to use new student housing facilities for conferences than students do. This new housing is more expensive than older dormitories, and if you live there, you may have to move out over holidays to make way for the conference crowd. If you do have to move out of your room when conferences are scheduled over Christmas and Easter breaks, you can usually store your luggage in a basement. Even if you are allowed to stay in your dormitory over the holidays, it will often cost extra. You'll probably want to use the holidays to travel or visit friends anyway.

Phones

For North Americans used to calling up friends to make, cancel, or confirm dates and appointments, the British (and especially the Irish) university is a rude shock. Don't expect a phone in your room. You'll be lucky to find a nearby pay phone allowing outgoing calls. If you share a flat off campus and invest in a telephone, specifically request an itemized bill from the phone company. Otherwise, make sure that everyone records the date, time, phone number, and length of conversation. Local calls are not free from a residential phone; every call counts. See chapter 9 for more information on the British/Irish phone system.

Housing—Wales

At two university colleges, Bangor and Aberystwyth, you have the option of applying for residence in a Welsh-only hall. At two other colleges, Swansea and Cardiff, you can choose to live on a Welsh-speaking floor in a dormitory. Living solely with Welsh students (and English students learning Welsh) has advantages and disadvantages. On the plus side, you learn a new language and culture and get a much better understanding of Wales; a better understanding, in fact, than many English students, who consider Wales another shire. "Don't worry about making friends," says a Welsh woman at Cardiff, "the Welsh like all foreigners except the English!"

On the down side, joining the Welsh-only hall means joining a very closed community. "In the North," claims an overseas student at Bangor, "separate halls make for separatism, and the Welsh are very insular." "Welsh students were tough to meet at first," explains an Aberystwyth American. "I didn't speak Welsh, and some people think you're an arrogant Englishman if you don't speak Welsh. But once they found out I was from California, they switched to English, and I made good friends. I didn't live in a Welsh hall, but I met many Welsh. If I'd lived in the Welsh hall, I'd have met even more."

Housing—Scotland

Most Scottish universities provide housing for freshmen (first-years). Be aware that Scottish first-years are younger (about seventeen) than English and Welsh first-years as well as North Americans studying abroad.

Housing—Ireland

Once again, *it's especially important to find your own flat in the Republic of Ireland*, unless you go to Trinity College Dublin, University College Dublin, University College Galway, or the University of Limerick, which have dormitory spaces for some overseas students, or unless you're on a U.S. study abroad program which arranges accommodation for its own students. If you are on a program, you may still want to find your own flat. Program housing often means apartments full of other North Americans. See page 41 for information on how to find your own flat or bedsit.

Many students in Dublin and Cork begin their year at the venerable Kinlay House, something of a legend among independent hostels. They're both centrally located and good places to overcome jet lag, meet fellow travelers, and get your bearings when you first arrive. Their addresses—Kinlay House, Christchurch, 2/12 Lord Edward Street, Dublin 2; tel. (01) 679-6644; and Kinlay House, Shandon, Cork City; tel. (021) 508-966.

UPON ARRIVAL

You'll arrive jet-lagged and tired and loaded with bags at some scrubbed, brightly lit, confusing airport in Britain or Ireland. For information on specific airports, and on trains and buses, see chapter 6, "Transportation", to determine which London or Dublin city station serves your university town. Directions to the university from the local train or bus station are often mailed to you before you leave home. Sometimes there are British or Irish students with cars or minivans to meet you when you arrive—and sometimes not (it's more likely if you're arriving in the autumn). Students in some North American college programs have their arrangements made for them, and there might even be an advisor on the airplane over. If you've applied independently and haven't received specific instructions from the university, check the college catalog for maps of the campus and town.

If you've been granted university accommodations, at your new *hall of residence*, look for your *porter* or *domestic bursar* (who will probably have an office somewhere in the building) and get your room assignment and keys from him or her. Since you'll likely arrive for a special orientation program a few days before the actual term begins, you may be charged a nightly fee for your room. Earlier in this chapter we discussed temporary housing options if you arrive having made no previous housing arrangements.

Registration with the Police

All non-EC and non-Commonwealth students planning to study in Britain for more than six months (or work in Britain for more than three months) *must* register at the local police station within seven days of arrival. If you're enrolled in a course for less than six months or working for less than three, this doesn't apply. At customs your passport will be stamped: *the holder is required to register at once with the police.* Registration is a whopping £36, and although you're expected to cart the bulky green card (certificate of registration) around at all times, you'll probably never need to produce it. To register, visit your local police station with your passport, two passport-sized photographs, and the fee.

In addition to registration, there are other regulations. For example, you must report every change of address to the local police station within seven days of moving, and you must report changes in marital status within eight days. Inquire about other regulations, and be warned: you can be fined up to £1000 for providing incorrect information. If you need to extend your stay in Britain, send your certificate and an explanation of changes to the Home Office, Immigration & Nationality Department, Lunar House, Wellesley Road, Croydon CR9 2BY, United Kingdom; tel. (081) 686-0688.

In Ireland, you're also required to register with the local police if you'll be enrolled in a course for more than six months, but it won't cost anything in the friendly Republic.

Registration with the National Health Service in Britain

In Britain your campus will have a university health center, where consultation with doctors is provided free of charge under the National Health Service as long as you're enrolled in a course of study for more than six months. You'll have to register with both an NHS doctor and dentist, and forms and procedures should be explained during overseas orientation. See chapter 8, "Health," for more information.

Orientation and *Fresher's Week*

Most universities provide anywhere from an afternoon to a week of seminars, talks, and welcome parties for overseas students. Many are directed toward all visiting students, but some are for North American JYAs only. During orientation you'll meet students from your home country and probably become good friends.

Orientation generally leads straight into *Fresher's Week,* when all first-year students arrive. This is a week of parties, bands, wild dancing, and drinking where you'll meet many students, including fellow residents in your dorm. Remember that the British and Irish students at Fresher's Week are beginning students and will be around seventeen, eighteen, or nineteen years old.

If you attend just one event during Fresher's Week, make sure it's the sign-up for club activities. The best way to meet British and Irish students is to sign up for clubs. Choices include Zen, archery, rugby, *Rag* (a social club which also raises funds for charity), and many more. If you arrive in January, it will be *your* responsibility to seek out information on these clubs—check the societies noticeboard in the student union.

During Fresher's Week you'll also meet your *personal tutor,* i.e., your academic advisor for your time abroad. Many students warn that this is the last time you'll ever see this person. For the most part, you will work out academic matters with the instructors.

4

What to Expect

Universities in Britain and Ireland are a lot like universities in North America. Students gather from different parts of the world to study their subject, meet others, socialize, and contribute to a diverse community. Yet while the basics remain the same, several aspects of student experience concerning academics and social life are unique to Ireland and Britain.

NOTE: This is the general introductory section for all universities in England, Wales, Scotland, Northern Ireland, and Ireland, though it particularly characterizes those in England.

ACADEMICS: GENERAL

The average North American university class proceeds something like this:

Bob walks into his large lecture hall at Mountain State University and chooses a seat among 250 fellow students preparing to take notes on contemporary politics. The professor, a dot on the horizon, starts talking and Bob starts writing. Once in a while someone interrupts to ask a question, but rarely—the room is too large. Fifty minutes later the professor writes on the board the reading and homework assignments for the next class. Bob joins in a communal groan as the professor announces a test in two weeks and lists some of the questions that may be asked.

In contrast, the traditional *Oxbridge* (Oxford and Cambridge) model of education of many English, Welsh, and Irish universities is more like the following (Scottish universities have a structure more similar to the North American model):

Jan arrives at her tutor's room with books in hand. It's mid-October, only two weeks into the term. "What did you read this week?" the tutor asks. Seating herself, Jan pulls out a book and describes her thoughts on a contemporary political writer. She recalls points raised in lecture and takes out her handwritten essay about the author and his book. The tutor asks questions, Jan asks questions, and the two have a fifty-minute discussion.

Some Obvious Differences

Class structure. Most liberal arts classes in Britain and Ireland consist of a lecture, held once a week with anywhere from ten to 150 students, and a tutorial, where one to ten students get together with their tutor to discuss topics in depth. Sometimes groups of students meet with their tutor for a weekly seminar, which is smaller than a lecture but larger than a tutorial. (In science classes, as in North America, there's also a weekly *practical*, or lab.) The most important part of your educational experience is the tutorial or seminar. These are more personal and intimate than lectures; you can ask questions, and you can argue and debate points in a small group where your voice is heard. Lectures—larger, more impersonal, and more like a standard North American university class—are frequently skipped. If you take first-year courses, you'll generally have more lectures and fewer tutorials. In upper-level courses, there are more tutorials and seminars, which is basically the same pattern as in North America.

Speaking in class. North American students are accustomed to speaking out in class and are often graded on their level of participation. However, in Ireland and Britain few students talk in lectures. As one student put it, "Everyone's going to stare at the American who raises a hand, and the lecturer will be unhappy because you're interrupting his flow." You are expected to speak in tutorials, but "...even there, a lot of British/Irish students just sit."

Professor versus lecturer. In Britain and Ireland you're generally taught by *lecturers*, who have the educational status of assistant professors in the U.S., or *readers* (Britain only) or *senior lecturers*, similar to associate professors. Lecturers don't necessarily have a Ph.D.; doctorates are earned entirely through original research, so they can take longer to complete than in North America. The term *professor* in Britain and Ireland is a privileged title, usually denoting the head of an academic department. One reason British/Irish lecturers enjoy exchange teaching in the States (and teaching U.S. students in Ireland and Britain) is that North Americans automatically call everyone "professor."

Textbook versus reading list. North American students are accustomed to learning their material from textbooks that neatly organize information into discrete, easy-to-follow chunks. Few British or Irish courses are textbook-based. Course content is defined by what's brought up in lectures and tutorials. British and Irish students usually get a reading list several pages long, suggesting books that might help students understand the material they're studying. You're not necessarily responsible for reading all the books on the list, mostly just those that interest you or that are specifically brought up in tutorials.

Three-term system. Most Irish and British universities operate on a three-term system, as opposed to the two-semester system common in North America. There are exceptions—the universities at Stirling, Galway, and Aberdeen are based on two semesters. The autumn term (sometimes referred to as Michaelmas or Martinmas in college prospectuses) usually starts at the beginning of October, the spring term (Hilary, Candlemas, Epiphany) at the beginning of January, and the summer term (Trinity, Whitsun) in the middle of April. There are generally two long vacations: Christmas break, for about four weeks, and Easter break, between spring and summer terms, four to five weeks. This is prime traveling time.

Computers. In general, word processing and computing facilities are nowhere near as accessible as those found at North American universities. There aren't as many copy centers or copy machines around either. British and Irish lecturers, unlike their U.S./Canadian counterparts, do not expect typed work ("but we're very grateful," notes one Scottish lecturer). You'll probably do all of your academic work, including papers, in longhand.

Spelling differences. Many words that sound the same when spoken by English-speaking people change from country to country (especially between Britain and the U.S.) when written down. Americans spell things more simply, and often more like they're pronounced. Such spellings may be circled in red on returned essays and are considered inappropriate in British/Irish education. The longer you're abroad, the more confused you'll probably get about spelling. Both the American *and* English will start to look just fine.

Some general rules:

American	English
...or (favor)	...our (favour)
...ize (organize)	...ise (organise)
...er (center)	...re (centre)
...am (program)	...amme (programme)

Some exceptions:

enroll	enrol
meter	metre—unit of length only, not the measuring device—e.g., the gas *meter*
phony	phoney

Americans-only courses. Some universities have established courses solely for students from the U.S. and Canada. These cover popular subjects like British history and literature, Shakespeare, or an area of local interest like writers of the West Country. While they can be fascinating and informative, these courses are more like package tours than British or Irish study programs. Some even arrange for minivans for jaunts through the countryside and stops at quaint pubs. The work load is minimal, and enrollment is limited to North Americans; it's not the way to experience British and Irish education or make British and Irish friends. Avoid these courses if you can.

Another worrisome trend is the proliferation of September seminars. North American students are asked to come three weeks early for a special "introductory course" that will supposedly earn them a number of credits and extend the short British/Irish term (which starts in October) into a full-fledged North American semester. The reality is likely to be more minibus tours and large groups of Americans.

Some Not-So-Obvious Differences

Structure. North Americans studying in overseas universities can feel lost, unsupervised, and unsure about how they're doing because there's very little continuous assessment. Your essays are discussed but not always graded; there are few exams, if any; there's no part of the textbook you must have read in order to know you're keeping up. "There's no structure!" say North Americans. "It's impossible to tell what my tutor wants." "I don't know how I'm doing, or what's expected of me." This is frustrating, disturbing, and can lead to various responses. Some students work twice as hard to make sure they're doing okay. Others become paralyzed with uncertainty and fear about their progress. Still others enjoy this system because it combines personal instruction with freedom over what to study. *You design your course, you provide your structure.*

Specialization. North Americans take drama, mathematics, biology, and art history in the same semester and no one blinks an eye. Such a course load is grossly unfocused to the average English, Welsh, or Irish student (less so to the Scottish), who has been studying the same subject for years. Taking an astronomy course would be considered a radical departure for a physics major. Even the most adventurous won't cross the arts/science boundary. If you're a science major, you take science classes; if you're an arts major, you take arts, the humanities, or social sciences (remember that you've applied to a particular department, not the whole university, so this focus is somewhat understandable). The English, Welsh, and those from Northern Ireland in particular come to university already knowledgeable about their fields, having decided their direction with their choice of A-level examinations taken in high school. Many North Americans in their junior year are still figuring out what they want to do.

Many lecturers want to be assured that you have the appropriate academic background for their classes before admitting you. Some

British and Irish advisors strongly recommend that you take all your courses in the same department, as your English, Irish, Scottish, and Welsh counterparts do. Yet taking courses in several departments, both in North America and abroad, lets you explore several areas of interest and see connections between disparate fields that may be missed otherwise. You'll also meet more people.

NOTE: The Scottish system is very different in terms of specialization. Students often spend four years at a Scottish university (as opposed to three at an English, Welsh, or Irish university) and have greater flexibility when choosing courses. In general, Scottish students spend their first year "shopping around," investigating a few areas of interest; they don't start focusing on major or minor subjects until their second year. This is more like the North American system ("although don't kid yourself, it's still a lot more specialized than back home," say students). In fact, the U.S. university system was heavily influenced by emigrant Scots.

Science versus arts. In general it's harder to get into science classes during a junior year abroad than into arts classes, unless you have the appropriate background. Science programs tend to be more rigid than those in the arts, humanities, and social sciences, with more stringent, inflexible requirements, but don't let that discourage you. You simply need a bit more preparation and legwork than students interested in other fields. Make certain that you have a solid foundation in preparatory subjects before applying for science classes overseas.

Nevertheless, North Americans seem to prefer arts courses (English, economics, history, politics, environmental studies) to science courses, unless they're studying abroad on a special exchange between science departments. Keep in mind, though, that some arts departments, especially languages, are as rigid as science departments about adequate background.

Elitism in the U.K. There are forty-one universities in the United Kingdom (England, Wales, Scotland, and Northern Ireland), but there are over three thousand colleges and universities in the United States. Only 6 percent of British students go to university (plus 7 percent to polytechnics and a few more to trade and vocational schools, making 14 percent overall) compared to over 60 percent in the United States. More students go on to university in Scotland, so the English, Irish, and Welsh numbers are actually even lower. Of course, many students at U.S. colleges spend the first two years catching up or correcting poor instruction received in secondary schools, while British students who actually do go on to higher education are somewhat better prepared for serious independent work. North American students accepted for a year at a U.K. university go during their junior year but often take first-year British courses because that's what they're qualified for even after two years of college. But the United States has an "education for all" philosophy as illustrated by the phenomenal growth of community and junior colleges, while the British (English and Welsh—the Scottish have a less elitist tradition, with 18 percent in higher education) still seem to be influenced by the traditional Victorian belief that education, and particularly higher education, is dangerous for the masses.

In the late nineteenth century, several *redbrick* universities were established for those from the upper classes in England, who were groomed for positions in colonial administration but unable to get into Oxbridge. Another 25-30 percent of the population were allowed only a basic education so they could function as clerks. The poorer half of the population received little education in the hope that they wouldn't notice their sorry predicament and revolt. In the 1960s this Victorian-shaped system was swept away in the fervor of student protest, a Labour government, and an inflow of badly needed cash. *New* universities, concrete architectural experiments at the outskirts of cities, were built in an appeal to open higher education to more people. This growth was put to an end in 1974, when then Conservative Education Minister Margaret Thatcher slashed funding for universities—a practice she continued with a vengeance as prime minister in the 1980s.

Despite the reforms, the educational system in England and Wales is highly selective and elite, and with only 14 percent of the population in higher education at all (one of the lowest percentages of any industrialized Western country), these students (especially in the sciences) have a better-than-average shot at getting desirable jobs, which reinforces their elite position. Adding to this elitism is the *grant system,* under which those few students lucky enough to be admitted to university got the government to pay their tuition and often their living expenses as well. The living grant (not tuition) dwindled fast under Thatcher and is being replaced by a U.S.-style *loan system.* In a country without a tradition of loans, university financial aid, alumni fund-raising, large endowments, or corporate support for higher education, the university system will have to demonstrate creativity and flexibility to make such sweeping changes work.

The contrast is fairly clear. The British (especially the English) tend to believe that anyone who scores well on their A-levels deserves higher education, paid for by the government. This is supported by the strong feeling on the part of most British that education is important for its own sake, that anyone capable of obtaining knowledge should be given the opportunity and the access to experts and facilities to do so. Americans tend to believe that education should be (and can be) available to almost anyone despite his or her background, and that its purpose is practical, with real-life applications.

NOTE: Polytechnics in England and Wales and central institutions in Scotland are doing much to brighten the picture, opening higher education to more people. Still, the elitism of university students is visible in their attitude toward polytechnics, which they often look down on. But considering the variety of courses offered and the number of students they attract, the polys, which are set to gain university charters in the next few years anyway, demand respect in their own right.

Elitism in Ireland. Irish universities are traditionally even more upper and middle class, especially Trinity College in Dublin, because there are fewer government grants than in Britain and you must be in dire poverty to get them. The Republic of Ireland began a higher education expansion program in the 1960s along with the U.K., evidenced by the modern architecture at the University Colleges at Dublin and Galway. Recently, some polytechnic-style *NIHEs* (National Institutes of Higher Education) have gained university status (i.e., University of Limerick and Dublin City University), opening educational opportunities to more students.

Grades and work load. The ABCDF grade system is generally not used in Britain or Ireland. Students receive a *first* if they're at the top of their class, followed by an *upper second,* a *lower second,* and a *third* (or *pass*). There is rarely a curve; if you get a 30 on a test, you get a 30. However, anything above 40 percent is usually considered a pass, as opposed to a cut-off of 65 percent in the U.S. and Canada. Grades from Britain/Ireland and North America generally correspond as follows:

Britain/Ireland		North America
First (70+ points)	→	A
Upper Second (60-69)	→	A-/B+
Lower Second (50-59)	→	B/B-
Third (40-49)	→	C/C-

There is no universally agreed-upon standard, however. Lecturers may write you a course evaluation, a few lines about your contribution to the class. Some British/Irish universities adapt grades to what they perceive to be the "North American system" and issue "American-style" transcripts, while some North American study abroad advisors work from their own interpretation of the "Irish/British system." If you're worried about grades earned abroad, take classes that aren't essential for your major, or check with your study abroad advisor about taking overseas classes pass/fail. Remember to save your essays and any graded work to show advisors and faculty members in the U.S. or Canada in case you encounter problems with credit transfer later on.

How much work you do at a British or Irish university depends on what you're used to in North America. There are generally fewer papers, tests, or homework assignments, and very little "busywork" overseas, but more reading, discussion, and emphasis on individual initiative in the learning process. You are not told which textbook pages to look over or what questions may be on the next exam. You decide which books to read and which essays to write, and you can voice your opinions in tutorials. For some this seems like a lot less work, and an easy year; for many it is a challenge.

North Americans don't come overseas just to attend classes, and Irish and British lecturers are aware that JYA students may go to France more often than to the library. "Well, I had five essays due my first term, but with all the traveling I only finished three. Still it didn't hurt my grade," notes one happy American abroad. Some students feel that grades are upped and missed classes forgotten, but all warn that if you spend all your time on a Greek beach, you'll fail just as you would at home.

Libraries. Libraries are a real sore point with North Americans used to early opening and late closing hours. Libraries in Ireland and

Britain offer restricted hours on Saturdays and are usually closed all day on Sundays. Students also complain about the difficulty of finding the books needed for their courses because, unlike the United States and Canada, few people buy their own copies, and most depend on the library's meager stock. You need to show your university ID to enter British and Irish libraries, whose collections are significantly smaller than those offered in libraries at many institutions back home. Don't expect hometown newspapers or familiar periodicals, except for *Time, Newsweek, USA Today,* and the *International Herald Tribune.* European journals and publications are, of course, well represented.

ACADEMICS: WALES

According to students, lectures are the norm, not the smaller and more personal seminars or tutorials. University colleges employ a part 1/part 2 system for most degree programs: part 1 is a year of general introductory courses in three subjects, and is followed (after first-year examinations) by part 2, where the student specializes in either one (single honors) or two (joint honors) subjects. JYA students usually have more flexibility than British students and can take courses in any subject.

ACADEMICS: SCOTLAND

The system in Scotland is less rigid and planned than the system in England, Wales and Northern Ireland, and Scottish students arrive at university after taking highers, not the more specialized A-level exams. Scots students spend their first year shopping around before concentrating on a chosen area of study in later years. The ordinary course (which most students choose) lasts for three years, and an honors course takes four years and requires more independent work. "When I came here I didn't know what I wanted to do, so this system is great," says a Londoner at Aberdeen. "In England you choose your field when you decide which A-levels to take. Here you can wait until your second or third year."

However, many North Americans feel that while the Scottish are less structured than other British universities, they're still more heavily structured than those in the U.S. and Canada. "This is not liberal arts," warns a Texan at St. Andrews. "There's no such thing as electives once you're into your honors subject." There is also less continuous assessment—"only a few papers and exams"—and according to many, "The professors (lecturers) are gods; Americans speak up but the Scots keep quiet in class."

Part of Scotland's long academic tradition includes an unusual university structure: the *rector* is the symbolic head of each university, elected by the students every three or four years. The rector can be anyone, from rock stars to political heroes to a popular tutor on campus. He/she is officially expected to run a complaints office, take ideas and suggestions from students, and function as the student representative with the administration.

ACADEMICS: IRELAND

As mentioned earlier, the fact that you are accepted by a particular academic department (faculty), not by the university as a whole, and usually restricted to courses within that department is a special concern in Ireland. "You're accepted by one faculty and basically stuck with its class offerings," although "you can always try to branch out." "Visit your personal tutor or academic advisor with a confident attitude and explain what you want to do. It just might work."

North Americans warn about the strong focus on end-of-year exams, coupled with a lack of continuous assessment throughout the year. "If you choose to be assessed by exam (or if you're forced to), your entire grade rests on your performance on a single three-hour final test!" explains an irate New Yorker at the University College at Cork. Some enjoy the freedom they get before exams: "This system really frees you up to travel at the beginning." Yet "it can freak the Americans out because they don't know exactly how they're doing, and there's often too much pressure at the end."

Irish university libraries are widely criticized by North American students, who claim that you can't find books, and if you can, you can't take them out. There's also a short supply of seating, queues, and limited hours: they close at 10:00 P.M. weekdays, 1:00 P.M. Saturdays, and offer no hours at all on Sundays.

Tutorials are part of many Irish classes, but North American students don't always realize that they ought to go. Tutorials may be led by grad students (postgrads) and are seen as unimportant "sections" or "discussion groups." Attend the tutorials: they're small and allow you to express your ideas and opinions and ask questions, activities which are frowned upon in the larger and more impersonal lectures.

UNIVERSITY LIFE

Student Unions

Each university has a union (*guild,* or *student association* in Scotland), which usually provides several bars serving cheap beer and pub snacks. The union may also house bank tills, the post office, a bookstore, or campus shop. There's usually a *welfare officer* to help with social problems (difficulties with landlords, emergency loans, recommendations of doctors, etc.), a *housing officer* to help locate off-campus flats, an *overseas officer* for visiting-student concerns (this position is not common at Irish universities), and an officer in charge of *ents,* or entertainment (bands, concerts, discos, and formal balls). The union is also the student political center of the university, where dedicated union types (who traditionally, but not always, lean to the left) engage in discussions over campus and national policy. Union officers are students elected by their peers; they take a full-year sabbatical, forsaking all classes in order to fulfill their duties and lobby the government on student issues.

In Britain, each university's union is automatically a member of the umbrella National Union of Students (NUS) unless most of the students in a given union vote to opt out (some students regard the NUS as an out-of-touch, "loony left" organization). In Ireland, the Union of Students in Ireland (USI) fills a similar left-wing political role for both Northern Ireland and the Republic, and several universities have already opted out. As an overseas student, you will find it's tough to get involved in union politics, because most union officers are elected the year before you arrive. Still, the NUS, USI, and most member and nonmember unions are interested in having visiting students add their voices to debate.

Club Activities

When you first arrive at your university, you can join any number of clubs and organizations, from antiapartheid and ballooning to yoga and Zen. Rag, which arranges parties, dances, marathons, and often annual hitchhiking races for charity, is one of the most popular. During *Rag Raids* mobs of students descend on unsuspecting cities to sell *rag mags* (photocopied magazines put together by Rag members). The *Rag Parade* involves a club-made float procession through town, while the *Rag Slave Auction* sells off students to be slaves for a day. Rag and other clubs are social and emphasize partying and entertainment. They're a great way to meet people. Sign-up takes place during Fresher's Week (as mentioned in chapter 3).

Cliques

Cliques form at universities the world over, but in Britain and Ireland they are often tied to academic departments as well as sports. Students arrive at their university having already decided what degree to shoot for. They take all their classes in the same department, know fellow students with similar interests very well, hang out with each other, drink in the pub together, and generally travel as a pack.

There is often a massive arts/science split: arts students see themselves as "interesting, fun people who smoke dope and go to gigs" and science students as "boring sods who squat in front of their computers"; science students view themselves as "serious people who have fun but also work hard" but arts students as "lazy tossers who have it easy." Arts snobbery in particular is reinforced by the traditional Oxbridge/Trinity College Dublin emphasis on arts courses.

The North/South split is also common, with "North" to an English southerner signifying anything above the Watford Gap, a service station on the M1 just north of London. Northerners are supposedly less well-off but more friendly, talkative, and interested in getting to know people than students from the South. Northern beer is also supposedly far better, stronger, and more flavorful than the weak southern brews. In Wales, the gogs cling more tightly to Welsh language and culture than the hwntws. In Scotland, there are countless other divisions, such as the legendary highlander versus lowlander; professional, Saxon Edinburgh pitted against diverse, Gaelic Glasgow; Scottish National party adherents versus southern English yahs.

On the island of Ireland, the North/South divide is more obvious than in Britain. The conflict in Northern Ireland began with religion and continues today as a secular political dispute. This book doesn't cover the current state of the division (or "The Troubles" as it's euphemistically described in Parliament and the press), but if you're interested in learning more, study abroad is the perfect chance to ask questions. *Be careful*. It's a sensitive issue and not everyone wants to talk about it. Generally, if you sincerely want to learn and if you ask people to explain before voicing any uninformed opinions of your own, you'll get a positive response (advice often unheeded by the English, who are extraordinarily ignorant about this situation so close to home). Approach the topic gingerly, and if someone (especially in Northern Ireland) doesn't want to discuss it, let it drop.

Americans are a distinct group at some universities, identified by basketball sneakers, jeans, torrents of permed hair, college sweatshirts, loud voices, and continuous smiles. Other standard cliques include the English *Sloane Rangers,* wealthy preps who wear *green wellies* (rainproof boots, similar in function and reputation to the L.L. Bean boat shoe) and shop in the posh Sloane Square area of London. *Ruggers* (or *rugger-buggers)* are into rugby; they're the campus jocks crowding pubs and shouting about girls and games (although the sport is becoming popular with women as well). *Gothics* dress in black, paint their faces white, and listen to hard-driving gothic music. Union *hacks* wear black too, organize marches to Downing Street or Leinster House, and get justifiably angry over education cutbacks and the Poll Tax.

Smoking, Alcohol, and Drugs

While antismoking sentiment and legislation have reached fever pitch in North America—with tobacco banned in restaurants, cinemas, and on every domestic flight—no similar fervor has taken hold in Britain or Ireland. Students smoke, even where signs warn against it, and many roll their own. North Americans are known throughout Europe by their "fanatical" ("but healthy!" say the Americans) opposition to cigarettes. The Republic of Ireland recently banned smoking in many public places (the only place on campus where it's allowed is in your lecturer's office), but this is the law, not reality. Expect your lungs to take a beating on both islands, and don't be surprised by incredibly young tobacco addicts, especially in Ireland.

Because the drinking age in the United States is twenty-one, American students are not accustomed to drinking socially in the more expensive bars and restaurants. At American universities you drink in sleazy bars that won't blink at your patently phony ID, or more often you join private parties in dorms or fraternity houses. Britain has a less prohibitionist attitude toward drinking, and the legal limit is a spottily enforced eighteen years of age. Ireland has the same age limit, but it is more likely to be enforced. University clubs and student unions see one of their roles as providing cheap beer for parties at campus bars or arranging crawls to local pubs in town. People drink to have a good time and they drink to get drunk (in Ireland, social drinking is considered about four pints per evening). Since pubs are so accessible, dormitory parties are infrequent and, at many universities, against regulations.

The pub is a comfortable place to hang out, talk, and socialize. There are problems when tanked students and locals simultaneously spill from their respective pubs after the 11:00 P.M.-12:00 A.M. last call. Avoid the top deck of a late-night double-decker bus, where fights may occur. North Americans can get into trouble because for some it's the first time they're able to drink freely in public, because it's their first experience in a culture in which there is no stigma attached to enjoying alcohol, and because North Americans are even louder drunk than sober. If you're not a drinker, there are low-alcohol beers and nonalcoholic drinks available, and there is surprisingly little stigma attached to passing up the pints.

While not as drug-fixated as the United States, awareness of the problems associated with drug abuse is growing in Britain and Ireland. You'll probably come across hash and marijuana, but harder drugs exist as well. Heroin is a particularly serious problem in the U.K. Though you'll hear frequent student references to wild weekends in Amsterdam (where they make a successful distinction between drug use and drug abuse), the police in Europe do not look the other way and may be especially hard on North Americans. Most importantly, drug abuse is not only criminal, it is a serious threat to your health. See chapter 8 for information on drug treatment.

Walking and Public Transport

One reason people are somewhat relaxed about alcohol use is that fewer students drive. Although some have cars, British (and certainly Irish) students aren't nearly as obsessed with the automobile as are North Americans. Cities and towns are designed for the pedestrian, with pubs and shops within easy reach; only Milton Keynes in England's Buckinghamshire, a modern, prototype city, is designed primarily for the car. Walking is an excellent way to learn about your area and to work off cholesterol-laden breakfasts. However, new universities are sometimes plunked in the middle of beautiful but isolated country settings, where buses, trains, and hitchhiking—not walking—will be the only routes to town.

Some city universities are scattered over a wide area, requiring students to use public transportation. Be aware that while several British and Irish universities market themselves as campus universities, their idea of a campus may differ from yours. "Campus" does not mean that the halls of residence are anywhere near the classrooms (or *lecture theatres*). "At home I'm used to rolling out of bed, pulling on sweats, and stumbling five feet to class, but here I've got to take a bus." A campus simply means that at least some academic departments are somewhat close to each other, and that there's probably a bit of grassy space between them.

Closing Hours

Most convenience stores, restaurants, and pubs close early by American standards. The bell rings last call in the English and Welsh pub at 11:00 P.M. Scottish and Irish pubs are open until midnight during the summer, and if you know a pubkeep, you may end up in a *lock-in,* a pub kept open long beyond what licensing regulations allow. But if you get a craving for food in the wee hours, don't expect an all-night Stop n' Shop, pizza available at 3:00 A.M., or twenty-four-hour Safeways. You'll find the odd late-night convenience store, but in general the pubs close at 11:00 P.M., the clubs at 2:00 A.M., and nothing stirs after that. On Sundays it's worse; liquor licensing is stricter and shopping centers often shut.

Sports Facilities

Britain and Ireland don't have the money to spend on running and bicycle tracks, large football stadiums, or Olympic-sized pools; facilities are basically unimpressive. Even professional sports grounds are sometimes outmoded and run-down. The ancient design and poor condition of Sheffield's Hillsborough Stadium contributed to a disaster that killed close to a hundred people in 1989. At a university you'll find good *pitches* (sports fields), tennis courts (many of them grass, after Wimbledon), and squash courts, but that's about it. If you want to swim, you may be limited to public pools available in some towns.

Popular university sports include rugby, football (soccer), badminton, and squash (never racquetball). Americans are heavily recruited for American football and basketball teams. "You're expected to have innate ability (especially in football) even if you weigh ninety-nine pounds, stand four feet ten inches tall, and have never touched a pigskin in your life!" Regular aerobics *(popmobility* in Scotland) are becoming popular, although nothing approaching the American fitness craze has hit the islands yet. Cricket, rugby, football, snooker, hurling, gaelic football, and golf are discussed in chapter 10. Other university sports include *abseiling* (rappeling or using ropes to climb down buildings) and *orienteering* (finding your way to an agreed-upon destination using only a detailed topographical map and compass). To use British and Irish sports facilities, you sometimes have to pay a fee to join the Athletics Union (AU) or Athletics Association (AA), and then smaller fees to join individual sports clubs.

A common North American complaint concerns the need to pay each time you use the weight room or courts, whether you're an AU/AA member or not. Some universities charge admission, even for teams participating in official competitions. You may be charged for your team *kit* (uniform) and other equipment, often at inflated prices. "The main reason American football hasn't taken off here is cost"—universities won't provide equipment and students can't afford it. A second complaint concerns how unathletic the British and Irish are. Teams generally meet for practice only once or twice a week.

FOOD

University Fare

One thing that North American and British/Irish students agree on is the quality of cafeteria cooking: "horrible." Although good vegetarian cafés exist on some campuses, few people look forward to standard fare like beans on toast in the morning, or soggy chips in the afternoon. As previously noted, students strongly recommend that, if given the option, you choose a self-catering hall or flat. You may be used to a regular meal plan, but just about anything you make yourself will be preferable to university food, so the loss of convenience is well worth it.

Traditional British/Irish Cooking

Architecture, literature, rock 'n' roll—these and a multitude of other activities and pursuits are performed with traditional British/Irish excellence and skill. Food is one monster exception. Suddenly you realize what drove the British away from home to travel the world and create an empire: they wanted a decent meal. But before delving into just how bad the food is, the shining exceptions should be noted.

☞ **Sweets.** British and Irish stores sell some of the best candy in the world, with Cadbury's, Galaxy, Fry's, Rowntree, and Mars as recognized national treasures. Popular and unique items include the Cadbury Flake, a brittle chocolate stick often stuck into ice cream (this is called a "99"). Snickers were once called Marathon Bars, and Opal Fruits are known as Starburst Fruit Chews in the United States.

☞ **Pastries, breads, and biscuits.** In most towns and cities you'll find bakeries selling an awesome assortment of cream slices, donuts, and fresh breads, all relatively cheap. Special Welsh breads include *bara brîth,* filled with fruits and nuts, and *laver* bread, made with seaweed. In Ireland, potato bread (or tattie bread) and *farls* are popular, the latter made with baking soda and buttermilk and available in wheat, soda, and treacle (molasses) varieties. Shortbread is a sweet Scots cookie made with flour, butter, and sugar. *Digestive biscuits* (or just *digestives)* are fantastic and coated with plain or milk chocolate.

☞ **Cream/milk products.** Dairy products are exceptional, especially those from Devon and Cornwall in southwest England. Milk is still delivered by milkmen. Pints are the standard size, and come in glass bottles and cardboard boxes. Larger quart sizes are available, but you won't find the huge plastic gallons you may be used to back home. Types of milk are distinguished by the color of the bottle cap: silver signifies pasteurized milk, red, homogenized, blue, skimmed; and gold, semiskimmed. Milk is sold fresh, but drink it fast because it spoils more quickly than milk at home.

☞ **Roasts.** The big Sunday meal with the entire family gathered around the telly to watch a game of football is the *roast*, a hunk of lamb, beef, or ham cooked for hours (sometimes hours and hours) and served with Yorkshire pudding (similar to popovers), vegetables, and the ever-present potato. It is filling and delicious, although like a lot of British food, about as light on the stomach as Fort Knox. Most bodies can handle this fare only once or twice a month.

☞ **Breakfast.** Everyone has heard accolades to the big British breakfast, the jewel in Britain's otherwise sparsely stocked food crown. It is as terrific and as large as folks say, although aside from the odd tomato or mushroom, french fries (chips), and beans tossed in alongside eggs, sausage, and bacon, it's really no different from what you get in most North American diners.

☞ **Tea.** The British and Irish love their tea. If you visit someone's home, they offer tea. If you visit someone's dorm room, they offer tea. If someone visits you, you should also offer tea, because it's a great chance to sit down and have a relaxing conversation. Afternoon tea is a tradition still adhered to, especially in south England, where you can duck into a teashop for scones, cakes, and cucumber sandwiches. British and Irish tea is strong and has milk added. If you want it straight, say so. In the West Country counties of Devon or Cornwall, you'll find the best cream tea, a pot served with scones and jam and the centerpiece—fresh, local, *clotted* cream, the consistency of marshmallow fluff. High tea, taken at about 6:00 P.M., is basically supper with a *cuppa*. Popular after a heavy lunch, it serves as a light evening meal.

☞ **Haggis.** Though not really a shining example of the best of British/Irish cuisine, haggis, the national dish of Scotland, should nevertheless be noted. Native Scots may tell you about their "haggis farm" in the Highlands, with all the cute little haggises running about on the moors. The reality is far more entertaining. Haggis is basically every part of the sheep that people usually throw away, all ground up and stuffed in the stomach. Yes, the stomach. For the best results, buy haggis fresh from a butcher's and boil it (the butcher can give you instructions). Eat it sliced and slathered in brown sauce (a mixture of a Worcestershire-like sauce and vinegar).

Now the down side. For North Americans used to gigantic plates of food, unlimited trips to the salad bar, and unending buckets of popcorn at the movies, British and Irish food is disappointing simply in terms of scale. Portions are small, side dishes don't come with a meal, and the British (and especially British Rail) cannot make sandwiches. You get exactly what you order, no more, no less. If you ask for cheese, don't expect to find any lettuce, tomato, onion, or pickle, only thin strips of cheddar between slices of bread. There's something called a cucumber sandwich, which is like ordering garnish on a roll in North America. The only real exception is the thick deli-type *stottie sandwich* served in areas surrounding Newcastle-upon-Tyne. The British (less so the Irish, who usually drop an extra potato or two on your plate) are notoriously cheap with food, and even McDonald's charges 6p for a packet of ketchup.

The operative words in British and Irish cooking are *potato* and *grease*. The British and Irish eat more of these items than any other people. Just about everything is fried (you can even get fried bread).

Potatoes are actually quite good for you, but grease is not. Fish and chips are the ultimate in potatoes and grease, and they taste great if eaten in moderation. In Britain, they are best up north, drenched with malt vinegar. There are few things more satisfying after a night at the pub. They used to be served in newspapers before the British and Irish discovered that potatoes, grease, and newsprint were even worse than potatoes and grease alone.

Something else you will occasionally find on the table in Britain is *black pudding,* a moist patty made of pork, fat, and blood—pig's blood. Like a wet hockey puck, and for breakfast no less.

Pub Fare

One of the best places for cheap and filling British and Irish food is the local pub. Pubs usually serve food from 11:00 A.M. until 2:30 P.M., and some also serve in the evenings from 6:00 P.M. until 7:00 or 8:00. Typical pub fare includes the *ploughman's lunch* (cheese or ham with bread, salad, coleslaw, and pickle), a selection of *pasties* (meat pies), *bangers and mash* (sausages with mashed potatoes), *toad in the hole* (sausage in a Yorkshire pudding), and *bubble and squeak* (fried mashed potatoes and cabbage), which makes some wild noises from the pan.

Transport Cafés and Sandwich Bars

Transport cafés are cheap, filling places to eat traditional British food (chips and egg, beans on toast, tomatoes straight out of the can) and European specialties (especially Italian dishes), while sandwich bars, found in major cities, are good places to grab a quick bite to eat and a drink on the go. They serve a variety of wrapped sandwiches and salads, and the better ones have soup.

Fast-Food Chains

Many British see the enormous growth of fast-food outlets as a sinister phenomenon and will lecture you on the polluting effect of American cultural imperialism—but they queue up in droves to eat there. Burger King, McDonald's, Kentucky Fried Chicken, and Pizza Hut abound, and homegrown copies like Wimpy's (famous for their spicy beanburger with cheese) and American Burger have sprung up in most towns. Unfortunately, in some areas they've replaced the fish n' chip shops, the traditional British fast-food restaurants. Most fast-food restaurants open early and close late, so they're popular with students for breakfast coffee and late-night snacks after the pub. Some U.S. chains are blacklisted among activists because they raise cattle on former rain forest land or serve food in styrofoam containers that harm the environment.

Ethnic Food

The blandness and limited variety of British/Irish fare are somewhat relieved by the abundance and spice of the ethnic restaurants found in university towns. In Britain, immigrants from former colonies and Europe have added their best to the cuisine (this is less true in Ireland). The best non-British food is Indian, and curries are chosen as often as fish and chips after a night in the pub. Curries are the most popular item on the menu: *vindaloos* are hot and spicy; *kormas* are creamy; *birianis* are spicy, but with their own distinctive flavor. Curries, vindaloos, kormas, and birianis come in chicken, lamb, and vegetable varieties. *Naan bread,* a large, oven-baked, yeast-based bread, is only one of the many appetizers to choose from. Once done with your meal, you can grab a few anise seeds, colored bits that pack a walloping licorice flavor. From Indian-owned grocery shops, you can buy *samosas,* crispy, spicy, deep-fried pastries stuffed with meat or vegetables. Chinese restaurants are everywhere and stay open late at night. Another ethnic food source important for students is the allegedly Greek but really Turkish kebab shops, with "mystery meat" (ham and beef minced and rolled together with fat) rotating on spits in the window. Kebabs are served in pita pockets. Watch out for the hot sauce.

DRINK

Beer

Beer is a classic British and Irish put-down of Americans. "Yank beer is piss." "That Budweiser of yours is crap." "Weak, mostly water." "I tried getting drunk on your beer once, but I spent all my time in the loo." Canadians get off a little easier, but the fact is that when you think beer in North America, you think pilsner—a light, chilled, carbonated concoction with plenty of froth. Get to Britain or Ireland and think again. Never walk to the counter and say "Gimme a beer." A Scottish bartender will answer: "Bitter, lager, real ale, brown ale, stout, porter, mild or heavy, half-pint or pint, and you're an American aren't you?" Beer is a lot more complicated in Europe.

To begin with it's served in pints or half-pints, so never ask for a glass or mug. In Britain, look round the rim of your pint for a small crown—the Queen's official seal of approval. Half-yards and yards don't exist in Ireland despite the fact that they show up in every Irish bar in North America.

The Big Five and Microbreweries

The big national companies that control many British pubs include John Courage, Whitbread, Newcastle, William Younger's, and Bass, Britain's largest brewer. They produce good beers, but it's often more interesting to sample the smaller local brews. The Cornish make New Quay, a steam beer similar to San Francisco's Anchor Steam. Tiny Harvey's in Lewes came out with a special beer to celebrate the twenty-fifth anniversary of the University of Sussex. Microbreweries in Britain are more common in rural areas (e.g., the West Country) where sales remain too unprofitable to be dominated by the national brands. A big exception is the London-based Firkin pubs, which serve their own brews fermented in the basement in large plastic tubs. The Dogbolter (5.8 percent) is one of the more lethal Firkin concoctions on tap. The Goose and Firkin by London's Borough tube stop is the original microbrewery and pub. For more information on microbreweries in Britain, contact the Small Independent Breweries Association, c/o The Jolly Roger Pub, 50 Lowesmoor, Worcester, England; tel. (0905) 21540.

Lager, Stout and Porter, and Ales

Lager is the closest thing to a pilsner from home, although stronger, and while local lagers are terrific, the brewing process is German and not what the British/Irish brew best. *Bitter* is very English, is served at room temperature, and is darker, softer, creamier, and nuttier than lager. It goes down easy; thankfully, it doesn't live up to its off-putting name. Yorkshire bitters, like Ruddles County and the rival brothers John Smith's and Samuel Smith's, are renowned. Part of the country's North/South divide is attributed to what are widely considered the North's far superior brews. Theakston's Old Peculier is a particularly powerful and unusual northern bitter—dark and flavorful and almost a stout. *Mild* is a light bitter, lower in alcohol and popular with Mancunians (people from Manchester). Scotland is well known for *heavy,* a brutal, powerful bitter. Its strength is determined from the numbers on the tap, which represent the former shilling tax that rose higher with increases in alcoholic content. Sixty is weakest, 70 up there, and 80-90 positively deadly. (In England and Wales the strength of beers is determined by the specific gravity often printed on the tap. Once into the 1040 range, you're talking strong.)

Stout is what the Irish brew best—a dark, thick, and creamy drink. The most famous example is Guinness, brewed at the St. James Brewery in Dublin, something of a national shrine. It should take at least five minutes to pour out a proper Guinness, leaving time for the microscopic bubbles of froth to settle. Sometimes the barkeep will swirl a clover leaf in the foam. Other popular Irish stouts include Murphy's, a sweeter drink, and Beamish. *Porter* is a dark beer similar in look to stout, made from precharred malt and fermented quickly at high temperatures.

The British in particular have a love affair with *ales,* heavier and sweeter than bitter, and brewed longer at warmer temperatures to give them more alcohol and flavor. Newcastle Brown Ale (or Newkie Brown) is probably the most popular drink on campus. It's made in the north of England in Newcastle-upon-Tyne and is mysteriously called "the Dog." In South Wales, Brains Special Ale is the strong and malty king. (The Duke of Edinburgh once gave a speech at the University of Wales, College Cardiff in which he claimed, "What this country needs is brains!" Students report that the response was suitably in the affirmative.) Aside from its great taste, Bass Ale is recommended for working wonders toward relieving that stopped-up feeling a few nights of indulgence can produce.

Real ales are brewed in their own cask to impart flavor and maintain tradition, and examples include Flower's and Samuel Smith's Museum Ale. Real ale made its remarkable comeback because of the efforts of the Campaign for Real Ale (or CAMRA), an organization that publishes *The Good Beer Guide* to real ales and the pubs that serve them: Campaign for Real Ale (CAMRA), 34 Alma Road, St. Albans, Herts. AL1 3BR, United Kingdom.

Whiskey

Both the Scots and the Irish excel in distilling whiskey (spelled *whisky* in Scotland). *Malt whisky* is made by a single distillery and aged for a certain length of time, while a *blended whisky* combines batches of whiskeys of different quality and age in the same bottle. Distilled from the fermented mash of grain (varieties include rye, barley, and corn), whiskey is *uisce beathadh* in Irish and *uisge beatha* in Scots Gaelic, both translating as "the water of life." Try not to drown, especially if sampling *poteen* (pronounced "pocheen"), Irish moonshine that's been known to lead some to blindness.

Cider, Scrumpy, and Snakebite

Cider, made from fermented apple juice, is a strong and popular alternative to beer; it's served sweet or dry. National brands are now available throughout Britain, but the West Country version, *scrumpy,* is the most powerful—sweet and smooth, and the cause of tremendous headaches. If you can find it, try *perry,* a similarly explosive pear drink. A potent cider derivative is the *snakebite,* which many pubs won't serve because of its notorious effect on the body. It's half cider and half lager, with a dash of black-currant juice thrown in. Replace the black currant with Southern Comfort and you've got a *rattler.* Some female JYAs warn that British men like to claim that the snakebite is a "ladies' drink" and really not that strong at all.

Wine Bars

Wine bars are now all over Britain (there are fewer in Ireland), particularly in university towns. They're popular with students, although some decry them as "yuppie, yah, Sloane Ranger" establishments lacking the character and atmosphere of a traditional pub. Wine bars are open later than pubs and usually serve lager along with various types of wine. Australian and New Zealand wines are probably a new experience for North Americans, as are expensive English offerings from vineyards in Devon, Cornwall, and East Anglia. English wines are celebrated with wines from around the world at the World Wine Fair held in Bristol each July.

Squash and Soft Drinks

Squash is highly concentrated fruit juice, although it's not always clearly marked as such. Never pour anything labeled "squash" into your glass and proceed to drink it; dilute a small amount with a glassful of water.

British/Irish Coke is a "soft drink with vegetable extracts" according to the can, but it tastes the same as Coca-Cola anywhere. Barr's *Irn Bru* (Iron Brew) is the Glaswegian alternative, an incredibly popular choice in Scotland, which tastes remarkably like Bazooka bubble gum in liquid form.

Water

The European Community is taking Britain to court for low water standards. High levels of aluminum, lead, pesticides, nitrates, and trihalomethanes have been detected in the tap water in some regions of the country. The government has simultaneously privatized the nation's water industry, leading many to fear that quality will drop further when the supplies are administered by companies out to make a profit.

5
Social and Cultural Issues

CULTURE SHOCK AND ADJUSTMENT

At first you're euphoric: I can't believe I'm here! A new country! Get a load of that black taxi, that double-decker bus! Listen to the way these people talk! A tutorial—I wish we had these at my college back home. Everything is new, interesting, and different. This is going to be great.

And then overload sets in. Britain and Ireland aren't quaint versions of the United States or Canada. Your head aches from trying to figure out the university system, banking, shopping, and even what the woman sitting next to you is saying. Your euphoria starts fading and gradually, everything new and different is a pain in the neck. You're embarrassed to ask people to repeat themselves; after all, it's in English, which you've spoken all your life! The food is getting on your nerves, the stores don't stock your favorite brands, and you're tired of cooking for yourself. Meeting new people and making new friends is wearing you down and you're beginning to miss the familiar structure and regular assignments of your courses back home. You can't even figure out how to find a doctor for the stomach problems you're having, and you miss your family, friends, the local sub shop, the late night convenience store, even the student cafeteria. That's when you know you've hit bottom—culture shock.

And you probably thought this wouldn't happen to you because, after all, you're not in Sri Lanka—you're in Britain and Ireland! This is Europe, the mecca of Western culture, adventure, and excitement. Everyone wants to come to Europe, and everyone has a great time. You should be ecstatic every minute! But be warned: culture shock catches almost everyone, although many don't recognize what it is, and it affects everyone differently and at different times. Some people skip the euphoria stage and go straight from jet lag to shock, and there are those who claim not to be affected at all.

The depression, frustration, exhaustion, and sadness that come from living in a new culture (or even in a new city or state back home) is a perfectly natural part of the adjustment process. After all, the familar people, support systems, and institutions have all been yanked from beneath your feet, leaving you standing alone in a strange and confusing land.

The important thing is not to try avoiding the discomfort of this phase but to recognize what it is—a natural process—and not fight or deny it. Culture shock takes many forms: exhaustion, headaches, insomnia, frustration, depression, a feeling of spinning your wheels but going nowhere, a desire to hide in the closet or in bed, a loss of appetite or memory, anger at unfriendly locals, inability to concentrate, loneliness—the list goes on.

When you start experiencing these feelings, slow down, regroup, try not to be so hard on yourself, and look after your physical and emotional health. Fighting the process will only make it last longer and will probably make it worse. And there are some positive steps to help pull you through.

One thing you can do (although it might be the last thing you want to do) is learn as much about your host country as you can. Instead of "Brit-bashing," seek out logical motives behind people's behaviors and attitudes, and behind everything in the culture that seems confusing, strange, or illogical. Look for patterns and relationships and keep an open mind. Read the newspaper and see what's going on. And strongly resist the urge to make jokes, nasty remarks, or hang out with unhappy Canadians or Americans; you'll only feel worse. You may experience the need to retreat and be with others from back home, and that is okay, but only to a point—your problem lies in trying to make sense of Irish or British culture, and spending all your time with North Americans can become a habit, and a bad one. Find a sympathetic British or Irish student or neighbor and talk with them about specific situations that bother or confuse you.

And finally, be patient with yourself, have faith in yourself—you will make it through. If you can look at your experience in Britain or Ireland as an opportunity to learn about a new country and about yourself, you will start feeling comfortable and be able to make the most of your time abroad.

BRITS, PADDYS, AND YANKS

Everyone holds stereotypes about other countries and cultures, and the British, Irish, and Americans are no exceptions. The British and Irish think that they know all about us from watching television and American movies. We don't know much about the British and Irish but why bother? They're just like us, right? Wrong! We share the same language, yes, but that doesn't stop us from totally misunderstanding each other.

However, many British and Irish know a lot more about Americans than we know about them and may delight in needling you about your ignorance of international affairs, inner city blight, homelessness, drugs, crime, you name it. "You get attacked as if you were personally responsible for everything from the slaughter of the Indians to U.S. policy around the globe," one student complains.

From "Dynasty"-style TV shows, the British and Irish easily reach the botched conclusion that "all Americans are rich, live in big houses, are not too intelligent, and are out for number one." Still, some of these stereotypes hit closer to home: they see us as inconsistent in foreign policy, regularly interfering in and exploiting small countries, and attempting to dominate Europe economically, politically, and militarily. And we're far too provincial and "America-centric." U.S. newspapers are filled with pages and pages of local and national stories, crowding out news from the rest of the world—which is too often reported on only when some disaster occurs.

Your best defense against these stereotypes is to arrive prepared and with a sense of humor. Learn about Britain and Ireland before you go. Read up on major U.S. and Canadian domestic issues as well as foreign policy and international concerns. When you encounter people who respond to you as a stereotype, be patient. They'll eventually learn to see you as an individual.

And don't forget that the British and Irish aren't the only ones who stereotype—you do this, too. Most Americans see the British as stuffy, class-conscious royalists with bad teeth, who eat fish n' chips, drink ale and tea, have quaint accents, and say "bloody" and "jolly good" around the house. And the Irish love green, wear shamrocks, drink Guinness, eat potatoes, celebrate St. Patrick's, and hunt for lepre- chauns among the clover.

Stereotypes are unavoidable. They help us make sense of our world, but they also make us squeeze people into categories, no matter how bad the fit. They color our perceptions so that we only see situations that support those categories. You will meet people that appear to be quintessentially British or Irish, but even these folks deserve a second or third glance—no one fits the mold exactly. Look at all people as distinct individuals.

CANADIAN STUDENTS

If you hail from the third-largest nation on earth, be forewarned: not only will the British and Irish automatically assume that you are from the U.S., many Americans will too! Militant Canadians take to wearing maple leaf patches on their packs and inserting "eh?" at the end of every sentence. Once their nationality is discovered, however, they report that their initial reception is often better than that accorded Yanks. Take the following exchange on a British Rail train, for example:

British:	"Where are you from?"
American:	"The States."
British:	"Oh…"
Canadian:	"Canada."
British:	"Oh! How nice! I've heard it's lovely!"

This has something to do with the fact that the British still emigrate to Canada, and many have recently transplanted relatives there. Also, warn Canadians, this treatment doesn't always last beyond casual conversation, but "it's not too bad if you're traveling by train."

Canadian students, however, have one major complaint about Brit- ain. The British (and especially the British press) tend to view Canada's current crisis as a split between "English" and "French" Canada, with the English side revering the Queen and cultural insti- tutions like pubs and high tea with a fervency that hasn't been evident in most of Canada for many years. "You'll see hilarious news reports noting Her Majesty's face on our money that assume we worship the woman or something. Sorry, but most of us couldn't care less, eh!"

MAKING BRITISH
AND IRISH FRIENDS

After six months or a year abroad, you'll probably leave Britain and Ireland with a real sense of sadness. The friends you've made overseas will be among the closest you have, and you certainly won't want to leave them.

It's often said that making British and Irish friends is difficult, yet once you know them, they're your friends for life. Both statements are resoundingly correct. Before you become friends, though, you have to work at making friends, and this can be frustrating. Americans and Canadians often claim that it's "hard to know" British and Irish students, but the truth is that it simply takes time. The process is slowed by clashes of culturally determined expectations and differences in what is considered ordinary or acceptable behavior when meeting and dealing with others.

Differences come in many kinds and sizes. Students from the United States smile a lot and are especially open, direct, and enthusiastic when they meet people for the first time, and this can seem phony and insincere. "Nobody's that happy," think some British and Irish. "I don't even know this person, what does she want from me?" While an American tells you his or her family history, medical problems, sexual frustrations, and work situation in the first five minutes of conversation, the British (and in particular, the southern English) are a bit more reserved. "Americans come on so strong it's intimidating, like they're trying to get the upper hand," claims an irritated Londoner. Americans are good at making frank small talk and tend to be incredibly nice to strangers. But this behavior doesn't necessarily mean anything beyond a transitory display of friendliness and courtesy. Just because you smiled and talked with some guy on a bus doesn't mean you'll ever see him again. The British don't understand how anyone can be that intense and then just vanish. To them it smacks of dishonesty and they don't trust it.

Another difficulty arises from the fact that North Americans often don't stay very long, many for only a ten- or eleven-week term. There isn't enough time to spend with British or Irish students, participate in clubs and classroom activities, or get to know people well. The Irish and British are aware of this: "Americans? They're from another country so there's all that much more to plow through," points out one Welsh student, "and they leave in four months."

Americans are judgmental, say many British and Irish. "This is dirty, oh how gross, you shouldn't smoke, I think that, I believe this, my opinion is." They act privileged: "It's the 'Won't you help me? I need assistance now, why isn't everybody waiting hand and foot' aura that surrounds some Yanks," explains an Irish student. "It's like everything has to be done for them right away." The American obsession with prompt, enthusiastic service ("Hi, I'm Dave and I'm your waiter for the evening") and the omnipresent "Have a nice day" are especially foreign to the Irish and British. Combine these tendencies with the strong American inclination to compare everything to how great it is back home and it's no wonder that some British and Irish are hard to get to know. Sure you shouldn't smoke, and Glasgow may be filthy, but imagine a visiting British student in New York City telling you that you talk too loud and moaning about how skyscrapers just aren't as impressive as England's cathedrals. Or a Londoner in Boise sneering, "What a backward village!" and going on about the incredible theater back home in the capital of the English-speaking world. You'd dump this jerk at the nearest corner and wonder why in the world she came over if all she wants to do is criticize.

Be aware that you are comparing things and try to tone down the more obnoxious comments. Remember that your expectations are culturally determined and not absolutes, and the way Americans or Canadians do things is not necessarily the best or only way to do them. You'll notice that British and Irish newspapers are often a lot thinner than North American rags, but look again: that *New York Times* is mostly advertisements, and what a waste of trees! When Americans encounter their first overseas fridge, they realize with a shock that it's not much larger than the one they installed in their college dorm. But while the American feels pity for the poor British or Irish who can't afford the space or money to purchase a "normal" refrigerator, the British and Irish sigh with pity at the North American who can't buy fresh vegetables every day and instead must store food for long periods in this wasteful, energy-guzzling box.

However, some British (in particular, some southern English) can be extremely arrogant, too. "I go to school in Wisconsin," you might offer, provoking a sneer of derision from a British acquaintance. "School? Oh, right, you Americans call university 'school.' Of course your universities are rather a lot like schools, aren't they?" Some of this is defensiveness, insecurity, and a longing for a now distant past. In Britain, the empire has faded, U.S. bases still litter the countryside, and the Royal Family is pop culture fodder for the sleazier tabloids. Yet you'll meet students unequivocally certain of Britain's prominence as the leading nation on earth. Americans who arrive with apparent confidence, cheery smiles, firm handshakes, and tales of massive cars and big fridges are extremely threatening.

Another reason both the British and Irish are difficult to make friends with concerns university housing. If you live in a dormitory, you'll be living with first-years, which means nineteen-year-olds (English and Welsh) and seventeen- or eighteen-year-olds (Scots and Irish). They don't take exams (at least not exams that matter), they always have free time, and many spend most of the year in the pub. North Americans on a year abroad are mostly juniors accustomed to living away from home, with fading memories of their own freshman experience. Some North Americans see the British and Irish as immature, while some British and Irish find North Americans too serious and stuck-up. Older British and Irish students are more mature, but they might already live off-campus with friends of their own.

Finally, it's just pure leftist chic to denounce America and to feign total disinterest in anyone from the other side of the Atlantic. If you're a U.S. citizen, you've got to expect an earful on the fact that your government is a conservative, ethnocentric clutter that has blustered and muscled its way around the world politically and militarily for a long time, made a mess of foreign governments and cultures, and has a mass of well-publicized problems at home. While most Americans jump at the chance to travel almost anywhere in the world, some British claim to have no desire to see the United States at all (the Irish are another matter: check the visa queues outside the U.S. Embassy). "All that commercialism, tackiness, insincerity. What is there to see?"

The trap that some fall into is allowing any initial distrust or difficulty to cloud future friendships. Again, it takes time to make friends, so keep talking, keep listening, and keep at it. Don't give up and hang out with that group from New Orleans. You came abroad to meet people and learn about the country, so work at making British and Irish friends. If first-years get you down, meet students your own age through classes or clubs. North Americans are easier to meet, so they often join foreign cliques, especially at universities that bring overseas students together before the term begins. Remember, a pack of Americans comes on stronger, louder, with even more teeth and handshakes than an American alone. It can't be stressed enough: *don't just make friends with other Americans.*

NOTE: In general, the farther you go from London, Dublin, and Edinburgh, the friendlier your reception. Londoners in particular are swamped by Americans and are tired of them crowding their subways and pubs. If you head for the countryside or a smaller city (plenty of fantastic choices are available), you'll be more interesting to the natives and more likely to gain acceptance. The Irish, in particular, are outgoing and less judgmental or prejudiced against Americans. With more Irish settled in New York than the entire Republic (forty million Irish-Americans across the U.S.), everybody knows someone or has a relative in the States.

THE IMPORTANCE
OF CLASS AND ACCENT

Britain and Ireland are inhabited by tribes, but the Angles, Saxons, and Celts of the past have given way to the *Brummies* (people from Birmingham), Geordies, Scousers, Gogs, Mancunians, and Cockneys of the present day. Each group is identified by language—accent, choice of words, manner of speech. The British and the Irish can place people the minute they open their mouths. The language generally reflects a continuing separation between those with vast amounts of inherited money and privilege and those who work at blue-collar jobs.

This separation of people by class remains intact, and you'll hear student union meetings hum with the terms "working class," "upper class," and "merchant class." The classes are not particularly fond of each other; for example, you'd rarely find an English boss hanging out with the office workers as you might in North America. However, Americans who claim they live in a classless society are suspect, given the European familiarity with television documentaries and books on America's growing and obvious under and upper classes. If you try to make a case for American egalitarianism, be prepared for a drubbing.

Oxbridge has traditionally been a kind of "accent academy," where the most unintelligible Welshman emerges with a voice fit for an audience with the Queen. However, the Queen's English has an irritating component to some—an effete, snobbish, condescending tone associated with the upper class. "A Scotsman leaves Oxford with no character at all," notes a study abroad advisor, with tribal disdain.

A short list of modern-day tribes:

- **Aberdonian** .... from Aberdeen
- **Brummie** .... from Birmingham
- **Cockney** .... East Londoner (usually working class)
- **Dundonian** .... from Dundee
- **Geordie** .... from Newcastle-on-Tyne
- **Glaswegian** .... from Glasgow
- **Gogs** .... South Welsh term for North Welsh
- **Hwntws** .... North Welsh term for South Welsh
- **Liverpudlian** .... from Liverpool
- **Mancunian** .... from Manchester
- **Manx** .... from the Isle of Man
- **Saesons** .... Welsh term for the English (Saxons)
- **Sassenachs** .... Scots term for the English (Saxons)
- **Scouser** .... from Liverpool

WORK ETHIC

Differing American and British outlooks on work and accomplishment are often illustrated by this well-known story. A man in a Lamborghini drives past a Briton and a Yank, leaving them both in his dust. The Briton fumes and yells "Bloody capitalist," while the American smiles dreamily and says to himself, "Someday, I'm gonna own an even better car than that!"

If there's one thing the British can't stand about Americans, it's their gung-ho attitude to get out there and live their clichés: squeeze the most out of life, make every minute count, go for it—in short, their infernal optimism that they can have it all. The British prefer the "you can't have everything" model. Slow down and go to the pub, not the gym. Life is about "making the best of a bad job" and "muddling through," not changing the world or worrying about succeeding or getting rich. The simple life is what it's all about: fewer possessions, but lots more free time. "Relax, mate."

MINORITY STUDENTS

Social Climate

First off, be aware that Britain and Ireland have relatively few minorities, although major cities in England (including London, Bradford, and Birmingham) have more substantial African and Asian populations. Minorities make up only 4.5 percent of England's fifty-six million people and are less common in Wales, Scotland, and Ireland. Of this number, half are of Indian or Pakistani origin, while one-fourth are Afro-Caribbean. Minorities are similarly underrepresented among North American JYA students, although African-American universities, notably Spelman College in Atlanta, offer rapidly growing programs. Spelman is an excellent source of advice for black students interested in studying abroad and can be contacted at the following address: Director of Study Abroad, Spelman College, Atlanta, GA 30314; tel. (404) 681-3643.

Britain has a diverse population, but compared to the United States, there's a fundamental difference in the way minority groups are seen. In the States you assume everyone, regardless of race or even accent, is an American. Your grandmother may speak with a thick Irish brogue, but she's still an American, and no one would question it. In fact, ethnic groups identify themselves with the national appellation: Italian-American, African-American, Japanese-American, and so on. The U.S. is a big country with a tradition of welcoming immigrants (at one time it had practically open borders), and everyone (except Native Americans) originally came from somewhere else. The old "melting pot" idea is being abandoned as the nation begins to acknowledge the mosaic of different cultures and the ethnic variety of American citizens.

British immigrants come mostly from countries of the former empire: Pakistanis, Nigerians, Kenyans, Ghanaians, Indians, West Indians, Malaysians, and others. Colonials were never expected to actually live on the small island (Britain) that ran the world, and their steady emigration has inspired disdain and resentment among many of Britain's "blue bloods." Indians running corner groceries and sending children to good schools are often perceived as Kipling's "White Man's Burden" and not valued for the extraordinary determination and energy they bring to the country; certainly they're not accepted as British. "I have nothing against the Pakis," less enlightened friends will tell you, "but if they're not going to learn our culture, they should go home." And you won't hear immigrants described as

Malaysian-Britons, or Indian-Britons; they are called Malaysians and Indians, still separate from the real British who fear the "Paki invasion" and, even more serious, a "Chinese invasion" when Hong Kong is handed back to China in 1997.

The British use the term "Asian" for everyone from Afghans to Japanese, and "Afro-Caribbean" instead of black or African to refer to immigrants from former Caribbean colonies who make up a substantial portion of the black population in Britain.

Minority Student Concerns

"Our minority groups are new," explains one British lecturer. "In the States there's a tradition of immigration, but immigration in Britain is a recent phenomenon" (this is even more true of Ireland, which has a far stronger tradition of emigration). "Blacks come here voluntarily," says another, "they didn't come against their will as they did in America. But their reception isn't always good. Some whites are scared, apathetic, uneducated. In the United States, you've had different races for generations. We British haven't had time to get used to different races." "They're bloody insensitive," claims a British Pakistani student at the University of Birmingham.

Racism (or *racialism* as it is called in Britain) is as rampant in the British Isles as it is in North America, and students report some blatant abuse. "This is more a problem with the general society," says an African-American at Lancaster. "You don't encounter major difficulties at the university, but I've got a black friend who couldn't find housing off campus because no one wanted to rent to blacks. It was pretty overt." However, "British students don't always see me as black, more as an American first, black second," he adds. "In that way I don't 'feel my race' as I do at home." "The British tell a lot of racist jokes," claims an Asian-American at University of East Anglia. "They are a lot more willing to use racist stereotypes in advertising, the media. I don't know what's worse, actually seeing the racism and confusion here outright, up front, or knowing it exists under a false coat of liberalism back home."

"In Ireland," says one African-American, "you can run across a bizarre response. OK, you've got your outright racists, but many Irish consider themselves to be 'the blacks of Europe' because they've always been downtrodden and discriminated against because of the English. So they feel that there's a link with American blacks, that we share something in common."

Among British minority students, the sense of living in a racist society is stronger. "We grew up here, so we've experienced the taunts, name-calling, and fights from an early age." "The worst thing is that white British students don't think there is any racism in Britain. It's saying that I'm lying about my own experiences." "The English like to feel it's class and accent that matter, not race," explains a British Pakistani, "so if you speak like a Brummie, you are a Brummie. But that's not true. I hear racist comments; people have said 'Paki' to my face." British police only began classifying attacks as "racially motivated" in the late 1980s, several years after residents in a number of English inner-city areas (including London, Birmingham, Liverpool, Bradford, and Bristol) rioted in 1984. British universities only started monitoring the race of those admitted in 1990, with the first question on ethnic makeup included on the Universities Central Council on Admissions application form.

The Rushdie affair (the publication by Penguin Books of Salman Rushdie's *Satanic Verses)* has deepened a split, especially in English cities like Bradford and London, between an offended orthodox Muslim community on the one hand, and Muslims and non-Muslims on the other, who are equally intense about preserving and defending the freedom of speech. Salman Rushdie was forced into hiding in early 1989.

Many, if not most, of the minority students you'll encounter at university aren't British or Irish at all, but overseas students from Africa and Asia pursuing graduate research in engineering, agriculture, chemistry, medicine, or international relations. Some are strongly dissatisfied with the way white British students treat them and consider themselves victims of racism. "They assume we don't speak English, and because we're a different color they don't talk to us at all." Partly as a result, overseas student clubs and societies are often very active and offer students from all backgrounds a chance to learn about other cultures and address minority concerns. They can be very separatist, too, but in general most minority groups (Afro-Caribbean, Chinese, Hong Kong Chinese, Lebanese, Malaysian, Pakistani, etc.) have popular university clubs that JYAs are welcome to join.

One organization active in the fight against racism in Britain is CRE, the Commission for Racial Equality. This government-funded commission was established in 1976 to investigate alleged areas of discrimination, including university admissions. CRE works closely with the nationwide network of local, voluntary Community Relations Councils, and you can write to the CRE for a listing of these councils.

Another helpful organization, the Institute of Race Relations, maintains a reference library at its London office with information on Third-World struggles and antiracism in Britain. They also publish *Race and Class,* a quarterly magazine. CRE and the Institute of Race Relations can be contacted at the following addresses: Commission for Racial Equality (CRE), Elliot House,10/12 Allington Street, London SW1E 5EH, United Kingdom; tel. (071) 828-7022; Institute of Race Relations, 2-6 Leeke Street, London WC1X 9HS, United Kingdom; tel. (071) 837-0041.

Other organizations you may want to contact for assistance are the National Union of Students, both in Britain and Ireland, the United Kingdom Council for Overseas Student Affairs (UKCOSA), and the Irish Council for Overseas Students (ICOS). All addresses can be found in appendix A.

GAY AND LESBIAN STUDENTS

Homosexuality remains illegal in the Republic of Ireland, despite the fact that the European Court of Human Rights struck down the law in 1989. From long before the election of the liberal Mary Robinson as ceremonial Irish president, there have been persistent calls for the repeal of this ban.

In Britain, sex between consenting males over the age of twenty-one has been legal since 1967, although Clause 28, which prevents the "promotion of homosexuality," causes anger and protest on college campuses. Lesbianism has never been illegal because HRH Queen Victoria couldn't believe that women ever did such things. Gay and lesbian societies exist on most British and Irish campuses, while city nightclubs and pubs offer special nights and promotions for gay and lesbian customers.

WOMEN'S ISSUES

Despite being governed for eleven years by a woman prime minister and possessing a female head of state, sexism is nevertheless no stranger to Britain. In Ireland, say many, the problem is even worse. The same pay and job discrimination that exist in North America is no less an obstacle in these countries, and laws guaranteeing adequate leave for women with newborns remain unwritten. While Margaret Thatcher was a powerful guiding force in British politics, there are few other women in either the House of Commons or the House of Lords.

Abortion rights are absent in the Republic of Ireland, where women still travel to the U.K. for the controversial procedure. At university, most of your lecturers will likely be men, and you might hear grumblings from women about needing a Y-chromosome to advance to a professorship.

Still, a strong and vocal feminist movement has promoted many changes in both British and even Irish society, and at university these have definitely taken root. Women speak up as often as men do in class and in general receive the same degree of consideration from lecturers. Women serve as student union officers and are active in most on-campus clubs. The notable exception involves sports: women are not always readily accepted in sports the British (and Irish) consider traditionally male, like rugby or football. Often separate sports with similar rules exist for female teams (for example, *camogie* is the women's version of the Irish sport of hurling).

6

Transportation

PLANES

Planes to London

Two main international airports serve London: Heathrow and Gatwick. Heathrow ((081) 759-4321) is one of the largest and busiest airports in the world. Its four terminals are easily accessible from two stops at the end of the Piccadilly line underground. Gatwick Airport ((0293) 28822) is a popular terminal for chartered airlines and flights to the Continent. British Rail Gatwick Express trains ((071) 928-2113) run every fifteen minutes to and from Victoria Station for about £6. The commuter train, which is slower and makes more stops, is a little cheaper.

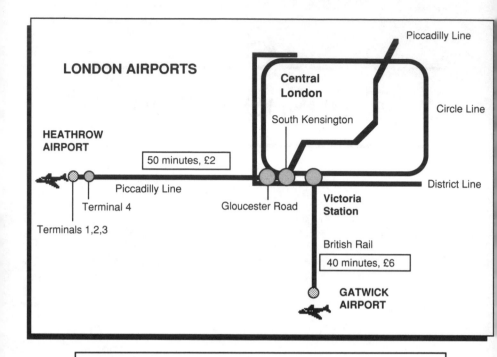

LONDON AIRPORTS

Piccadilly Line

Central London

Circle Line

South Kensington

HEATHROW AIRPORT

50 minutes, £2

Piccadilly Line

District Line

Terminal 4

Gloucester Road

Victoria Station

Terminals 1,2,3

British Rail

40 minutes, £6

GATWICK AIRPORT

Other London Area Airports

- **Luton Airport** ((0582) 36061)
  mostly flights to the Continent

- **Stansted Airport** ((0279) 502380)
  a new airport for international flights

Other Planes to England

Students heading for the Midlands can fly into Manchester Airport ((061) 489-3000) from New York (on British Airways), Chicago (American Airlines), or Toronto (Air Canada). There are also occasional charter flights from other North American cities. A bus leaves the airport every half-hour for the thirty-minute ride into town and costs about £1.50. Manchester is also a major hub for flights to Continental Europe.

Planes to Scotland

Glasgow Airport now accepts direct flights from the States on well-known carriers such as American Airlines, British Airways, and Northwest. A bus departs from the airport every half-hour for the twenty-minute trip into Glasgow city center, where you can catch a train or bus to your final destination.

Planes to Ireland

Students attending Irish universities have two choices. Dublin Airport (01-379900) is in the east of the country, and flights are met by a bus to Dublin city center which stops at every stop on the way to Busáras, the main bus station near the Customs House, for about IR£1. There's also a direct coach to Busáras for around IR£3. Shannon Airport (0353-6161444) is outside Limerick (return bus fare IR£4) in the west of Ireland. Aer Lingus from New York and Boston services both airports.

Peak, Shoulder, Basic, and Off-Peak Fares

Plane fares vary according to season. Peak fares are the most expensive and occur during high seasons (holiday times such as Christmas, Thanksgiving and Easter), when traffic flow is heaviest. At the beginning and end of each high season, airlines offer shoulder fares which are less expensive than peak but more than basic prices. During months when traffic flow is steady, airlines charge a basic fare, and off-peak fares are reserved for low periods when few people travel—usually March and July. Accordingly, flights from North America are cheaper if you leave in January for university spring and summer terms, as winter is off-season for cold and wet destinations. Some of these fares are amazingly cheap, particularly Virgin Atlantic. Autumn-term students pay more because London is popular and dry in the fall.

Ticket Types

☞ **Advanced Purchase Excursion (APEX).** APEX is the official airline discount fare with up to 60 percent off the regular cost of a flight. Because of the restrictions, though, this option usually works better for visitors than for students. You must reserve a ticket two to

four weeks in advance, and you may be required to take your return
flight within four to six months. The tickets are cheap, and if you're on
a short course, APEX may be the best way to travel. Pex or Super Pex
flights are similar to APEX but can be booked closer to your departure
date.

☞ **Charter flights.** A good bargain for students at popular flight
times, charter flights are cheap and don't require that you return right
away. However, you must choose your return date when you book the
flight, and this date is final. Any change (especially within three weeks
of your flight home) may result in the loss of your money. In addition,
charter flights aren't 100 percent reliable, and your plane can be
cancelled two days before departure. They are also notoriously
overbooked, so get to the airport early, and expect lines.

☞ **Standby.** Flying standby is not a great choice because you won't
enjoy guarding the ton of luggage you'll be carrying overnight or
returning to the airport day after day, hoping to get a seat. Whoever
helps carry your bags or drives you to the airport won't be pleased
either.

☞ **Round the world fares.** These are terrific bargains if you get a
hankering to travel the globe after six months in Lampeter (it happens) For about $1200 you got a ticket for seven or eight destinations
worldwide, to be visited during a single year; for example, Montreal-
London-Delhi-Bangkok-Tokyo-San Francisco-Montreal. The first
stop on your journey must be booked three weeks in advance, you
can't backtrack (e.g., go London-Delhi-Paris-Tokyo), and you arrange
subsequent air tickets as you go along. You might even consider
booking a round-the-world flight from home, spending six months
studying in Britain or Ireland, and then continuing off to tour the
globe.

Cheap Airlines, Budget Travel Agencies, and Bucket Shops

Some of the cheapest airlines going are Air India and Air New
Zealand. Their spicy curries and kiwi desserts are definitely preferable
to "chicken or fish," and for the price, these carriers can't be beat. Book
weeks, even months, in advance. They often have special one-way
deals, mostly from New York, and the round-trip fares (about $450)

are terrific for family and friends planning to visit. As previously noted, Virgin Atlantic Airways is another good option, with flights from JFK, Newark, Miami, and Los Angeles into London Gatwick. They offer especially low fares during off-peak periods.

These deals aren't always available directly but must be purchased through budget travel agencies specializing in cheap flights (some are reserved for students only, so bring along your ID). For a list of budget travel agencies, see appendix E.

You can also check the classified sections of newspapers and "what's on" magazines for *bucket shops* (cheap travel agencies specializing in student flights), which offer spectacular discounts, mostly on charter flights. Be wary, however; some bucket shops are semi-fly-by-night outfits and less than meticulous in their business operations.

Courier Flights

Scheduled airlines are best for hauling bags at the beginning and end of your stay, but the cheapest route to other countries or home for the holidays is through a courier company, which charges very little for most flights. Fares as low as £150 round-trip London to New York, or £200 London to Seattle are not unheard of. You give up your baggage allowance and take only carry-on bags (although on many routes your baggage is allowed), and the company ships its parcels (usually documents or computer software) in your name. A courier company representative meets you at the airport, checks you in, and gives you the paperwork required by foreign customs. You meet another representative at the end of your flight and hand over the paperwork. You're not responsible for what the company ships.

Courier companies appear and disappear all the time, but British companies that have been around for a while include Courier Travel Service (CTS), Polo Express, and Nomad Courier Fights (see appendix E for addresses).

Courier companies also run flights from major U.S. cities like Los Angeles and New York. Relatively dependable companies include TNT Skypack and Polo Express. Check the Yellow Pages for listings.

Airport Security

It is important that you get to the airport at least two and a half hours before takeoff and expect everything electronic (Walkmans, cameras) to be thoroughly checked. You may have to play your radio or take a sample Nikon snap. Nothing electronic (this includes Walkmans) is allowed in your carry-on bags. Airport officials/agents are particularly interested in gifts you were given by other people to take overseas, so be prepared to list them. Security is serious business at international airports, and no one finds bomb jokes appropriate or funny. A standard announcement at Heathrow Airport in London is, "Please keep your baggage with you at all times. Unattended baggage will be removed immediately and may be destroyed." They're not kidding either.

TRAINS

Britain

British Rail (ScotRail in Scotland) is the national rail network, linking most cities and towns in the country by fast but expensive service. Intercity trains run up to 125 miles per hour and are generally efficient, but local service varies. Delays and cancellations are the lot of the British, who stomach difficulty with admirable ease. You'll fume in your seat as the train slows into another deserted field and you get to view sheep and cows without a railway station in sight, but your fellow passengers will simply flip through the pages of the *Daily Telegraph* or *Sun*. There is one inflexible rule you must follow when dealing with British Rail or risk, as posters warn, a "criminal record": *buy your ticket before boarding the train, and keep it until the end of your journey.* Some students don't buy tickets to avoid paying for their ride, but this is a risky move. You can be asked for your ticket when boarding the train, while riding on the train, and when leaving the train, and if you don't have it with you, you're breaking the law. According to one ad, Sally was a respectable housewife until she cheated on her fare. "My life is ruined," she cries as she is hauled away by the police. Some honest students report rude treatment from British Rail personnel who take these advertisements very seriously, slowly scanning tickets for evidence of fraud. This happens most often near university towns and major tourist destinations where young people gather.

You'll probably use the train enough to warrant the purchase of a Young Person's Railcard, which gets you, if you're a student or under twenty-four (bring proof!), one-third off the regular price of each ticket for a full year. Railcards are available from any BritRail station, although you may as well get your railcard at the airport when you arrive and start saving on that first trip to your university. The price is around £16, and there is often a £5 discount at the start of the autumn term. You'll also need two passport photos (photo machines can be found in most stations). During one month each year, usually February or November, BritRail runs a special deal for holders of the railcard, setting the top fare for anywhere in the country at only £14. BritRail also sells a Disabled Persons Railcard, which entitles the holder to one-third off the regular ticket price.

For European travel, a good bet is the Inter Rail card, which is sold in every European country but cannot be used within the country of purchase. While you must technically be a local resident (for at least six months) of the country that issues you the card, some student travel agencies ignore the restriction. *But remember: European train guards check your passport, and if they're not satisfied that the card is valid, you may end up walking home.* The risk is yours.

Inter Rail is generally cheaper and more extensive than the Eurailpass, which can only be purchased in North America. The Eurailpass, like Inter Rail, also covers countries in Eastern and Western Europe and includes train travel in Ireland but not in Britain. The standard Eurailpass provides unlimited travel for one or two months. However, Eurail now offers a Youth Flexipass that allows for either fifteen or thirty days of second-class travel over a three-month period. This is a huge improvement over the standard Eurailpass, which tends to promote fast and furious travel in order for students to get the most value out of the high-priced pass. The BritRail pass (one month of unlimited travel) is for Britain only, but like Eurailpass, it must be bought before arriving overseas.

A standard single ticket is good for a one-way trip for three days from the date of purchase. A standard return is a round-trip ticket good for three months, and it costs twice as much as the standard single. Period return or saver tickets are valid for one month and cost less than a standard return, although restrictions on time and date of travel often apply. A cheap day-return ticket is the least expensive round-trip ticket you can buy, but you must leave and come back on the same day.

NOTE: Watch out for the doors on some British Rail trains. There may be no handle on the inside. If the door seems impossible to open (and you need to open them fast at the occasional four-second stop), pull down the door's window, reach out and turn the handle on the outside.

London Train Connections

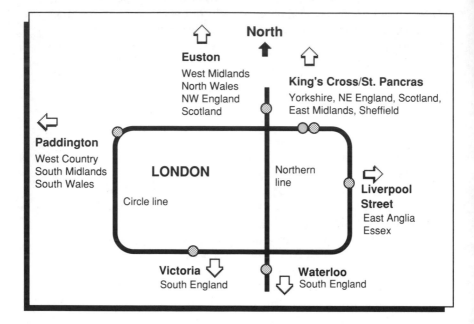

The Underground

The Underground, or tube, provides commuter rail service within London and the surrounding suburbs. It's a vast but easy-to-understand system, with eleven separate, color-coded lines covering much of the greater London area. It's also the oldest underground system in the world, with all the attendant problems—crowding, delays, decay, advertising, and graffiti—of a big city metro. Londoners are often stunned to find an escalator (some still made of wood) that works. Smoking was finally banned on the system after a disastrous 1988 fire at King's Cross Station left thirty-one people dead, but you may still encounter the odd cigarette. A series of broadsheets called "Poems on the Underground" are interspersed among the advertisements and give the tube a unique local touch. Like British Rail, you must keep your ticket until you reach your destination. Fares are based on how far you travel, and the system is divided into five zones. Zone 1 covers most of central London. You can buy a single ticket for each ride or a Travelcard (daily, weekly, monthly, yearly) for unlimited travel on London's tubes, trains, and buses. A Young Person's Railcard gives you a small discount, but only on the one-day Travelcard covering all five zones.

Real people used to check tickets at tube stations, but electronic gates now handle this task. There are few things more annoying to a Londoner than an American blocking the entrance while figuring out the gates (the only thing more annoying is the gate itself), so learn the system fast. Excellent maps of the tube system are available free from any Underground office. For more information call London Transport Travel Information: (071) 222-1234. See appendix E for a map of the Underground.

There are less extensive tube systems in Glasgow, Liverpool, and Newcastle-upon-Tyne. Remember that tube and underground are the right words for this kind of transportation. A *subway* is a pedestrian underpass.

NOTE: Anyone traveling from Ireland to Britain can get rid of excess Irish coins in London Underground ticket machines. The 10ps and 50ps should both work. (This applies to British pay phones, too.)

Ireland

Iarnród Éireann is the national rail network of the Republic of Ireland, covering all university destinations and hooking up with Northern Ireland Rail (NIR) at the border town of Dundalk. Ireland's rail system is not comprehensive, unless you're traveling to and from Dublin. Several journeys require stopovers in the capital city.

If you have an ISIC student card, pick up a *travelsave stamp* from USIT, which gives you 50 percent off the cost of a single (one-way) ticket and 30 percent off the cost of a return. The travelsave stamp offers the same discounts on buses, all for only IR£8. Although the stamp is probably your best bet, Iarnród Éireann also offers the Fare Card, which gives you 50 percent off the price of any rail ticket, single or return; bus fares are not discounted. Bring proof of age, a passport-sized photograph, and IR£8 to any Iarnród Éireann station or travel center if you want this card: Iarnród Éireann Travel Center, 35 Lower Abbey Street, Dublin 1, Ireland; tel. (01) 363333; or 65 St. Patrick Street, Cork, Ireland. Union of Students in Ireland Travel also sells the travelsave stamp; see appendix E for address.

Dublin Connections

There are two main train stations in Dublin, covering separate areas of the country:

Dublin Train Stations

- **Dublin Heuston Station**
  Dublin 8 (on the Southside, beyond the Guinness Brewery along the River Liffey): tel. (01) 365420, Monday-Friday; tel. (01) 365421, Saturday-Sunday
  Serving Limerick, Cork, Waterford, Galway, Killarney

- **Dublin Connolly Station**
  Dublin 1 (on the Northside, at the end of Talbot Street off O'Connell Street); tel. (01) 365418, Monday-Friday; tel. (01) 365419, Saturday-Sunday
  Serving Sligo, Belfast, Rosslare Harbour, Derry

BUSES/COACHES

Britain

Buses travel local routes through cities and towns and are often double-decker. The best seats are on the top floor toward the front, although it's good advice to stay off the top floor late at night when the pubs close. As noted before, if there's going to be a drunken brawl, that's where you'll find it.

Coaches are long-distance buses traveling between cities and towns and are cheaper than trains. National Express is the largest company and covers the most routes, although it's now being privatized and broken into parts, making for confusion. The double-decker Rapide coaches serving all major cities are comfortable, with reclining seats, toilets, and full-length movies provided on board. A Student Coach Card, valid for one year, gets you one-third off the regular price of each ticket. It costs £4.25, and you'll need two passport photos to buy one. You can purchase National Express tickets at coach stations throughout the country, at National Express offices (in London at 52 Grosvenor Gardens and 13 Regent Street) and at WH Smith bookstores. Other companies place ticket agents in bus stations in the areas they serve. As on trains, you must buy your ticket before boarding. The conductor can sometimes sell quick-issue tickets, but on a tight schedule he might not have time. If he's late or feeling grumpy, you'll probably be left behind.

Although cheaper, coaches are much slower than trains. Getting out of London and other large cities is a major hassle, with rush hour traffic beyond belief. The average speed in the English capital is 11 miles per hour, only 3 miles per hour faster than in 1911, when horse-drawn carriages filled the narrow streets. Once on the motorways, things improve, but commuter routes can be crawled faster.

London Connections

Coaches in London leave from Victoria Coach Station ((071) 730-0202), a few blocks south of the Victoria Tube stop along Buckingham Palace Road (you must exit Victoria Station to reach it). The National Travel Office in the station sells tickets and can help you with timetables and bookings.

Ireland

Bus Éireann is the national coach company of Ireland (their optimistic symbol is a racing Irish setter). The Irish are more likely to take coaches than trains; they are direct, cheaper, and serve more destinations. But they are also agonizingly slow, and the rides are bumpy. Irish highways are like backcountry U.S. state roads. Service is often infrequent: "Watch out for Sundays," warn students, "when few buses go anywhere at all. The bus drivers are either in church or in the pub—or both." Expressway coaches (newer ones are nonsmoking and completely without legroom) travel between cities, provincial buses ply the local routes, and private companies cover the major tourist areas (Glendalough, the Ring of Kerry). Dublin Bus ((01) 734222) runs the capital city's commuter routes, and Bus Éireann handles local services elsewhere in the country. Remember that an express bus in Ireland is one that makes ten stops instead of fifteen.

USIT issues the travelsave stamp to holders of the ISIC student card. IR£8 gets you 50 percent off all one-way fares and 30 percent off the round-trip (the travelsave stamp also gives you similar discounts on trains). For scheduling information for the whole country, contact Busáras Enquiries, Store Street, Dublin 1, Ireland; tel. (01) 366111.

FERRIES

The cheapest student method of travel between Britain and Ireland (and between both islands and the Continent) is ferries, which regularly ply the rough and British submarine-infested waters of the Irish Sea. You have a choice of train or coach for the overland part of your journey. The train is faster and easier to sleep on, while the coach costs less. Buy a ticket for the entire journey from the train or coach company you choose. It costs more if you purchase the ferry passage separately.

Overnight journeys are a draining but popular way to avoid overpriced airlines and youth hostel costs, but be warned: the seats are designed to be incredibly uncomfortable, with armrests and barriers and no place to sleep (ferry operators want you to crack and choose their expensive berths). If you are prone to seasickness, take dramamine an hour before leaving port, and try lying flat (on the floor, under tables, or in the space between seats); it settles the stomach. Just ignore overweight British and Irish travelers trading in graphic puke stories while liberally consuming their duty-free. If nothing works, console yourself with the fact that the Irish Sea is one of the roughest bodies of water in the world, so what did you expect? For a list of major ferry operators and a chart of approximate travel times for popular routes, see appendix E.

One good tip: bring an orange or apple (or both) for the morning you arrive. It helps to replenish lost moisture and vitamins and gives you a little energy to start the day.

HITCHHIKING

Hitchhiking is the most exciting, informative, and definitely the cheapest way to travel and learn about a country. Britain and Ireland are small islands you can cross in a day by train, clacking past fields and factories for a few hours with your luggage precariously stored above your head—or you can spend days or even weeks exploring back roads and countryside in other people's cars. Sure you've heard tales about vanishing hikers and seen occasional tabloid horrors and *The Hitcher;* Rutger Hauer in a Mini is a scary thought indeed. Yet hitchhiking is legal (except on motorways, or major highways, although you can travel them by hitching from entrance ramps), relatively safe, free, and a common way for students to travel. You meet great people; learn about jobs, troubles, current events, and history; hear terrific stories; and develop a feel for the way a country works. Hitchhiking is most effective for one man, two women, or a man and woman traveling together. Other combinations wait longer. *A woman should never travel alone.* In case you've never hitchhiked before, here are a number of other rules to follow:

☞ **Don't hitch in a hurry.** It's possible to go halfway across the country faster than your average bus, but hitching usually requires that you take your time. You need patience, but waiting is not a bad thing. An hour on the asphalt lets you stretch out and think; a ride miles out of your way can take you to a ruined castle. If you're after speed, stick to the motorways (although even they become slow-moving and congested because of frequent road construction), but don't set a schedule or you'll be frustrated and late.

☞ **Pack light and pack warm.** You won't see station wagons or space shuttles on wheels in Britain or Ireland, and external frame packs are tough to cram in a Mini. A small pack gives you a much greater chance of success. But don't skimp on sweaters, jackets, or long underwear. It gets cold, even in summer.

☞ **Hold a sign.** Write out your destination on an old piece of cardboard or a strip torn from a box. Let drivers know where you're going, even if it's Llanfairpwllgwyngyllgogerychwyrndrobwllllantysiliogogogoch (a small town in Wales). Or make up destinations; for instance, write "Disneyland" and draw a mouse to intrigue or at least get a smile from a driver. It might help to add "please" or a question mark to your sign, too.

☞ **Look neat.** Why do drivers stop their comfortable cars and let total strangers in the front seat? Probably because they're tired or want company and see you as a safe, decent, interesting young person with a sense of humor. Wear a good shirt and jeans, shave, comb your hair (the more conservative the cut, the better, although you'd be surprised how many people with paisley mohawks get rides), stand straight, and smile.

☞ **Act.** Few drivers will pick you up if you squat by the side of the road looking bored. Hitchhiking is taxing because you've got to want this ride, even if it's the 500th car you've seen that day. Sing a little, stretch, run in place. If someone waves, wave back, give a thumbs up, and take comfort in the fact that it's a reaction—you're not ignored, you've made contact. Smile! Clutch your heart and plead if the car is about to pass. Get on your knees and pray to a Volvo. Be creative, and you'll get lifts.

☞ **Check out the driver.** If the ride doesn't seem safe to you for any reason, if it's a kid with a thirty-year-old car and acid house music blaring from octaphonic speakers, or if Rutger Hauer actually does pull up in a Mini, don't get in. Another car will come, really.

☞ **Talk.** Nobody picks you up so you can crash out and snore. This is a chance for both you and the driver to learn something. Ask about hitchhiking, local issues, what he or she thinks about the United States or Canada, and any towns or interesting places you pass. After a five-hour haul from Liverpool to London, you might end up exchanging addresses and visiting the driver's home.

It is illegal to hitch or walk on the motorways; the police will stop and fine you. As noted above, however, you can hitch from motorway entrance ramps and from service stations. But the Queen's gift to hitchers is the roundabout, a traffic circle routing cars in different directions off a central track. These are everywhere, forcing approaching drivers to slow down and yield to vehicles already in the circle. Look for roundabouts, for they guarantee a steady stream of slow-moving cars going the way you want. Stand by your exit from the circle, put out a thumb, raise your sign, and smile.

A good map is essential for successful hitching, and the American Map Corporation's *Travel Atlas of Great Britain and Ireland* does the trick. It's light, comprehensive, compact, and opens flat to each page.

General maps of the major British and Irish motorways which you will most likely use for hitching are provided in appendix E.

EUROPEAN TRAVEL

The Continent is just a ferry ride away, and many North Americans take advantage of that proximity and travel to Amsterdam and Paris every other weekend. Regularly leaving the campus for European visits reinforces the British/Irish stereotype of the wealthy and spoiled North American (particularly those from the U.S.). Save your travel for vacations; appreciate and explore the country you're in, and make British or Irish friends during the term. Over Christmas and spring breaks (when conference groups might force you out of your dormitory anyway), don't be ashamed to go crazy: explain to critics that this is your best (and possibly only) chance to travel in Europe and that living in Nebraska does not afford the same opportunities to cross foreign borders. Also realize that Irish and British students in North America are no different: they see everything from the Golden Gate to Key West on cheap Greyhound and Amtrak passes, the same way you'll cover territory from the Aegean to the Arctic Circle with your discounted Eurailpass or Inter Rail.

You're likely to meet European students during the term, mainly French and Germans in England and Norwegians in Scotland. Once you make friends, you could end up spending the holidays in Paris, Berlin, or Oslo!

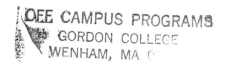

7

Money and Banking

CURRENCY

The United Kingdom

Money in the U.K. is called *sterling*. One hundred *pence*, or *p,* equals one *pound* (also known as a *quid* or *nick*). The tiny, silver 5p (formerly one shilling) coin was reintroduced in response to legitimate complaints about the weight of British change, and both the newer 10p and older two-shilling coins are still equally acceptable. The 20p, vital for drying loads of laundry, is also in circulation. Currency is divided into the following denominations:

U.K. Currency

Coins: 1p, 2p, 5p, 20p, 50p, £1
Banknotes: £1 (in Scotland), £5, £10, £20, £50

NOTE: Irish coins and bank notes are *not* accepted in the U.K.

Ireland

In the Republic of Ireland coins come in the same denominations (except for the £1) as in the U.K., although the size, color, and design all vary. The Irish pound is also called a *punt*.

Scottish and Northern Irish banks retain the right to issue their own legal tender, but if you try to use it in some parts of England, prepare for laughter and quizzical looks; it may not be accepted, particularly notes from Northern Ireland. You will meet with less amusement if you try to use Irish Republic bank notes in Northern Ireland; you may even provoke an angry response. Southern Irish currency is emphatically not accepted. British bank notes are generally acceptable anywhere in Britain or Ireland (as long as the exchange rate remains favorable for Irish merchants!).

BRITISH AND IRISH BANKS

British and Irish banks, which have no U.S.-style tradition of huge college tuition loans, nevertheless offer a number of services tailored to student needs. These services include student accounts, student services officers, campus branches, and (by U.S. standards) an incredibly calm and flexible attitude toward overdrawing an account.

The main banks in Britain and Ireland are as follows:

Northern Ireland	Scotland
Northern Bank	Royal Bank of Scotland
Ulster Bank	Bank of Scotland
	Clydesdale Bank
Republic of Ireland	England and Wales
Bank of Ireland	National Westminster
Allied Irish Bank	Barclay's
National Irish Bank	Lloyds
	Midland

They are called *high street banks* because they traditionally maintain offices on main streets (called high streets in Britain and Ireland). They generally employ a student services officer at campus branches and offer other special services, although many of these are for British and Irish students only.

Despite these special student services, banking can be an enormous headache for North American, British, and Irish students alike. English banks in particular charge for everything, from simple forms to withdrawals over your daily limit, especially if you're not at your own branch. "These charges are arbitrary," declares one high street teller, "and they vary from branch to branch." One student with an account in London tried to withdraw money over his limit (which can start as low as £50/week) from a branch at the ferry port in Dover. It cost him £10 and two hours to get official approval faxed from London to Dover—and he was withdrawing £10! You don't have to be a foreigner to encounter these difficulties. The banks are equally imperious with home students. Especially in London, don't be surprised if you're treated like a crook every time you go in, if you have to pay £3 for a blank withdrawal form if you forget to bring your checkbook, or if every cashpoint (ATM) within a four-mile radius is out of cash. Outside London, however, you can expect friendlier and more helpful campus or local branch personnel, fewer outrageous service charges (although there will still be charges), and an on-campus student services officer to answer specific concerns. In Ireland, banking both in and out of Dublin tends to be the same—friendlier service with fewer hassles or charges than in Britain.

Cashpoints

Cashpoints are found at many bank branches and remain open twenty-four hours a day. Students warn that "they never have money when you need it," much like the ATMs back home. Banks have reciprocal agreements, allowing you to use your card in cashpoints belonging to other institutions. Ask about this when you get your card.

Opening an Account

If you're on a study abroad program, the program or university may have an arrangement with a specific bank and will tell you how to proceed. Otherwise, you have two choices: open an account before you leave or upon arrival.

Before leaving. To open an account from home, write to the campus branch of the bank you choose, which will instruct you on how to proceed (your university can usually give you names and addresses of banks near campus). Some universities and study abroad programs do this for you.

Upon arrival. To open an account once you arrive, bring your passport for ID and, if possible, a letter of recommendation from your bank manager back home. If you'll be abroad for less than six months, you should tell the British or Irish bank (more important for the British) you'll be in the country for at least a year; otherwise, you may have a real hassle trying to open any account at all.

There are two general types of bank accounts to consider:

Current account. A current account is a noninterest-bearing checking account. Cash is easily accessible with a cashpoint card, although checking services are limited: checks will not be accepted unless you present a bank-issued check guarantee card, which can take over six months to obtain. However, a current account does allow you to pay bills by mail, which may be helpful for students renting flats.

Deposit account. A deposit account is an interest-bearing savings account. It is usually used for storing large amounts of money you won't need immediately. If you withdraw money without giving seven days' notice, you could lose interest (although it's generally not a significant amount).

The current account is still probably better for most overseas students than a deposit account because there's no penalty for suddenly withdrawing large amounts of cash.

NOTE: Closing an account takes anywhere from five to seven working days to accomplish, so don't wait until the morning of your flight. You'll have to turn in your cashpoint card and arrange a date for picking up your money.

Student Services Officer

Most bank branches near or on a university campus employ a student services officer to help handle student accounts. While not students, these officers are supposed to understand the trials and tribulations of university life as well as facts about attending the local university, including housing, tuition, living expenses, etc. You'll meet the student services officer when you visit the bank to open your account. Student services officers decide if you qualify for an overdraft, a loan, or a check guarantee card, and they can help you if you suddenly find yourself in dire financial need.

Overdrafts

Going into overdraft means withdrawing more money than you have in your account. Unlike North America, where a bank will skewer you for being a dollar overdrawn, British and Irish banks expect students to have a negative balance from time to time. Overdrafts are very popular with students and many leave university with big ones.

U.S. and Canadian students are eligible for overdrafts, but the bank knows you're fleeing the country at the end of term and will be reluctant to lend you cash. If you do go into overdraft, expect charges, but compared to North America the fees are small. Try not to go into overdraft without first making arrangements with the student services officer at your bank.

BRINGING AND SENDING MONEY TO BRITAIN AND IRELAND

When you arrive in Britain or Ireland, as mentioned on page 36, you should have with you approximately two hundred dollars in local currency (remember that traveler's checks, even in pounds, aren't widely accepted as cash) to get to your university, buy your first meal, and take care of any immediate necessities. There are a number of options for getting money to Britain or Ireland.

☞ **Take traveler's checks with you or have them mailed.** This is one of the best ways to take money to Britain and Ireland, in pounds or in dollars (pounds are best in order to avoid hefty commission charges overseas). Deposit them in a bank account as soon as possible after you arrive (save a few for travel or emergencies). Mailing traveler's checks is risky, but when it works it's the cheapest way to send money abroad. If they're in dollars, you'll pay commission to cash them at a bank but not at an office of the company that issued the checks (American Express, for instance).

☞ **Have money mailed to you in a cashier's check.** Your own North American bank will be happy to issue you a cashier's check, an official document that is as good as cash, or so the banks will promise. Actually, you will have to wait up to six weeks while the British or Irish bank clears it with your bank at home.

☞ **Telex or cable money through a large bank.** Once you've opened your overseas account, send your account number, the bank's address, and the bank's *sorting code* to your North American branch (or your parents, or whoever is handling your finances). Money is transferred directly from your U.S. or Canadian bank branch to your new account in Britain or Ireland in about one week, and it costs around $35.

Sending money is fastest from a big city main office. When you contact your local branch and ask them to send money overseas, the branch first notifies its main office, which then notifies its international agent. The agent notifies the main office of a bank overseas, which sends your money to the branch you request. If you bank at the Hog Farmers COOP in Des Moines, this can take a long time. If you bank in Chicago, it will take less time.

☞ **Send it through the mail as a money order.** A money order works well only if drawn on a bank which has a branch in Britain or Ireland where you can cash it directly. Otherwise, it's no better than a cashier's check and requires months to clear.

☞ **Wire it.** It usually takes three days to wire money to an American Express office and three to four days to a British or Irish post office through Western Union. If you're after speed, Western Union now offers the "Will Call" service that allows a student to pick up money at a Western Union office in Britain or Ireland within fifteen minutes of a call from North America. The toll-free number is (800) 225-5227, and the sending party pays by credit card. This is by far the fastest way to send money abroad, but you pay for the convenience ($42 to Western Union for any amount under $500).

☞ **Withdraw it from your North American bank account through a British or Irish cashpoint.** Certain U.S. banks that belong to the "Plus" system will allow you to withdraw up to £50 at a time through a British or Irish cashpoint. The rate of exchange is never clear, and the British or Irish cashpoint can't give you your account balance back home.

☞ **Use your credit card.** You may be able to get a cash advance on your credit card, up to your credit limit, from a bank. In shops and restaurants, Visa is the most widely accepted plastic, although many places take American Express, Access/Eurocard/MasterCard, and Diner's Club, too. You will be charged at the exchange rate on the day the bill arrives at the bank that handles your credit card, not on the day you make your purchase.

Lost Credit Cards: Britain and Ireland

Visa: Northampton (0604) 230230
American Express: Brighton (0273) 696933
Diner's Club: Farnborough (0252) 516261
Access/Eurocard/MasterCard: (0702) 338366

☞ **Cash personal checks with American Express.** If you have an American Express card, you can cash personal checks from your U.S. account at American Express offices worldwide, without paying a service charge.

THE BRITISH POLL TAX

The Poll Tax is the most hated tax in history, and although it is scheduled for repeal, the process will take at least two years. You'll hear a lot about the Poll Tax in Britain, and it will affect anyone studying abroad here for more than six months: *overseas students are required to pay 20 percent of the Poll Tax.*

The Poll Tax, or *Community Charge* as the government likes to call it, is a tax on people, not property, income, or anything most governments usually consider taxable. When the British leave school at age eighteen, they're automatically sent a bill for local community services, which in its first year in England and Wales ran as high as £700. As pointed out in debates everywhere from the streets to the House of Commons, the last British poll tax was repealed in 1381, after violent public protests. New protests filled Trafalgar Square in the center of London during an anti-Poll Tax riot in the spring of 1990.

The Poll Tax replaces the *rates,* property taxes that were high for those owning large estates and lower for those renting flats in the inner cities (renters sharing flats used to divide up the rates, or they were factored into the rent). The Conservative government scrapped the rates system in favor of the community charge, so that the United Kingdom became one of the few Western countries without a property tax.

The amount of Poll Tax people pay depends on where they live; their local council sets the rate based on the number of services (garbage collection, libraries, homeless shelters) it provides. People in wealthy districts often choose private health and education, so there are fewer local services and they don't pay much, while people in poor areas who survive on community services are forced to pay the most. The only person exempt from the charge is also the richest woman in the world, the Queen.

As mentioned above, students (including overseas students in the U.K. for more than six months) are expected to pay 20 percent of the Poll Tax. The amount varies from campus to campus, with the maximum tax around $280, or £140. How payment is handled varies. Some universities now ask for it along with tuition and housing fees and do the paperwork for you. Others let you receive the local tax forms and deal with it yourself. If there's no Poll Tax information on the application form, or in any subsequent mailings from the university, after you arrive speak to the JYA or overseas student advisor or the overseas and welfare officers at your student union for advice on what to do.

The Anti-Poll Tax Movement

Over a million people refused to pay their Poll Tax after its introduction in Scotland, and an antipayment campaign began the day the charge was introduced in England and Wales. The Conservatives tended to lay the blame for the tax's unpopularity on agitation by left-wing groups like Militant and the Socialist Worker's party (SWP), but antagonism ran deep among Conservative voters as well.

Nonpayment is still a serious offense, but it's seen by many as a form of civil disobedience. Several less drastic avoid-the-Poll-Tax schemes did crop up, including investing in a Cornish tin mine. Under a royal charter granted in 1508 by Henry VII, anyone with a financial stake in a tin mine is not liable for English tolls and taxes. The Conservative government was not amused by this ploy. Because the community charge is a tax on individuals, collection has been a real headache (collecting property tax was easy—a house wasn't about to get up and run away). If you do not pay your Poll Tax, your local council may take the following four steps:

1. Send out several ominous letters asking for payment.
2. Deduct the amount owed (along with heavy fines for nonpayment) from your salary if you are employed. If you're unemployed,

they can deduct it from your spouse's salary, take it from your welfare check, or even freeze your bank account.

3. Seize your property. They can take valuable items (your television, refrigerator) and sell them at warrant sales to recover the tax. (In Scotland the *scumbusters,* mobile citizen squads equipped with CB radios, organize anti Poll Tax protesters to protect other nonpayers' homes against any sheriff who comes to seize property.)

4. Put you in prison.

NOTE: You are strongly advised to avoid any anti-Poll Tax political or protest activity. It's an issue for the British to deal with, not outsiders, and breaking the law may cost you your right to remain in the country.

8

Health

BRITAIN

There are two types of care available in Britain—private and the National Health Service. Private means that you or your personal insurance covers the full costs of any treatment you receive. NHS care is funded by contributions from employee wages, so you pay only minimal charges or no charge at all. Doctors, dentists, opticians, and specialists are permitted to provide either type of care at their discretion, and you can be a private or NHS patient, depending on your eligibility for NHS treatment.

Before you read on, become acquainted with these terms:

general practitioner (GP)	doctor
surgery	doctor's office
chemist	pharmacy, with a pharmacist
consultant	specialist
casualty department	emergency room

The National Health Service

The National Health Service has been the cornerstone of the British welfare state since the 1940s, when Prime Minister Clement Attlee determined to provide British citizens with "total care from the cradle to the grave." An ambitious goal to say the least, and while you're in the U.K. you'll hear many opinions on whether or not his plan has actually succeeded.

At one time, the NHS was held up as a model of comprehensive health care for the rest of Europe—free doctors' visits and prescriptions, free eye tests and dental work; even hospital bills were covered. Yet with every tug of war between Conservative and Labour governments, the NHS has been stretched and cut, leaving services overworked and underfunded.

With the Conservatives at the helm, the NHS faces its greatest challenge for survival. The government wants to shift as much health care into the private sector as possible. In the United States we are used to outrageous private medical costs, but the shock waves caused by dismantling socialized medicine in Britain are rippling through every medical organization and social welfare group in the country.

What this means to you is that your local clinic or GP may be unclear or completely unaware of what sort of care you qualify for as an overseas student. So, be prepared and, above all, keep a healthy attitude. Even better, keep healthy.

Personal Medical Insurance

It is a wise idea to get personal medical insurance before you leave home, regardless of how long you plan to study. If you'll be in a course for less than six months, you probably won't be covered by the NHS. Without personal medical insurance, you'll have to pay private health care fees for treatment, and it is extremely expensive. Even if you'll be in Britain for more than six months and are covered by the National Health Service, it is safest to carry personal insurance because there are long waiting lists for some medical procedures and some people express concern about the quality of NHS care.

NHS Eligibility

The Departments of Health and Social Security (DH and DSS, formerly known collectively as the DHSS) are government agencies that oversee the operation of the NHS and set the guidelines for NHS eligibility. By law, any ordinary resident is eligible for NHS coverage. The exact definition of this term, however, is controversial with regard to foreign students.

According to the U.K. Council on Overseas Student Affairs, a 1983 court case established that any student in a full-time course in Britain for more than six months qualifies as an ordinary resident and is covered for NHS treatment from their first day in the U.K.

NOTE: For male students who are married or have children, accompanying dependents are also eligible for NHS care. However, British immigration law prevents female students from claiming their husbands as dependents, so NHS qualification for them is out. Sexism lingers on.

How to Get NHS Care

First, you should visit your university's health center before you get sick. Depending on size and facilities, the staff will either register you with their own on-campus GP or recommend several local GPs who are used to treating their students. You can also get a list of local GPs from the post office, library, or local Family Practitioner's Committee, which are all listed in the phone book.

You must register with a GP in your immediate area, usually within a mile of where you live. Unlike U.S. doctors, most British GPs operate out of a group practice, with several GPs using the same surgery. Registering with a group practice means you can take advantage of more flexible surgery hours and fit your visits around your class schedule.

Some students say that once you register with your local GP, you're automatically treated as an NHS patient, without filling out forms or being in a six-month course. The government wants to believe this is the exception to the rule. Generally, it depends on arrangements made by each university with local GPs and clinics and on the GPs themselves.

You will need to be treated as an NHS patient. Your GP will probably check that you are a full-time student intending to stay in the U.K. for at least six months, then ask you to fill out an NHS application form, which he or she will submit on your behalf. If your paperwork goes through, you'll be given a medical card with a National Insurance number that provides access to NHS treatment from your local doctor as well as from local NHS clinics, specialists, dentists, eye doctors, and hospitals.

NOTE: If you have a BUNAC work permit when you enter Britain and you manage to find a job, you'll be treated like any British employee. National Insurance contributions will be deducted from your wages, and you will be fully covered for NHS care during the six months the permit is valid. The exception is for anyone entering the country with a preexisting illness. In this case, your local GP decides how you pay for treatment.

NHS Coverage

Once you qualify for NHS care, most standard medical services are covered, including free consultations with your GP, home visits, access to family planning clinics, VD treatment, travel vaccinations, casualty services, and emergency hospitalization for accidents and illnesses that occur in the United Kingdom.

Treatment varies for long-term medical conditions such as diabetes or heart disease. *If you'll need special medical care during your stay, notify the university about your condition before you leave home.*

Hospital care. There are both private and NHS hospitals, and some NHS hospitals have private wings. If you qualify for NHS care, you can use the NHS hospital. Theoretically, there isn't any difference in the quality of care, but NHS hospitals are notorious for long waiting lists for nonemergency operations and patient complaints about shortage of staff.

If you become seriously ill, it might be a good idea to check into private facilities. This is where your personal insurance becomes vital; private hospital beds in Britain can cost over £300 a day. Your GP is your best resource if you have a serious illness. He or she can recommend a specialist who may also be part of the NHS.

Emergency services. Emergency services are provided free on the NHS, but even if you are not registered, you won't be turned away. They will treat you first and ask questions later. *A warning: what Americans consider an emergency and Britons consider an emer-*

gency may be two different things. Car accidents and appendicitis are emergencies. Hangovers, stress attacks, sinus infections, bad colds, and stomachaches are not. Not all hospitals have emergency wards. Make sure you know which one in your area does.

Dentists. The British tend to have a collective national fear of dentists. Europeans in general aren't known for healthy teeth, and the thought of a dentist's drill makes even the toughest "lager lout" tremble. Somehow, this fear is passed on to overseas students, and horror stories about experiences with British dentists abound. "They're still in the Dark Ages." "They took out my front teeth for no reason." "I wasn't given any anesthetic." "My roommate had the wrong tooth removed."

Fortunately, dental care has changed. Treatment is being modernized and more attention is given to preventive care than in the past. But some students find the financial pain even more horrifying than the physical. Even on the NHS, you still pay 75 percent of the high costs of tooth decay.

You can find out about local dentists through your GP, post office, library, or local Family Practitioner's Committee. You are not restricted to a neighborhood dentist as you are with your GP, but you must specifically ask for NHS treatment when you first visit your dentist. Dentists assume you'll be a private patient because the NHS covers so little.

For routine checkups, prices vary widely, depending on where you live. For complicated work, the dentist should give you a cost estimate after your first consultation and work out a deposit/payment schedule as treatment progresses. Unlike GPs, dentists can refuse to treat you as an NHS patient—and they might, because if they treat you privately, they're not bound by any set scale of fees. You may want to shop around.

Eye care. In April 1988 the government introduced a charge for all basic eye tests in Britain. Depending on where you live, they cost anywhere from £8.50 up. The only people exempt from this charge are full-time *British* students under nineteen, social security recipients, or people with special conditions such as diabetes or glaucoma. You'll also be charged for lenses and frames (which used to be free), with or without a National Insurance number. Low-income groups (this could mean you) can apply to the DSS for vouchers to help pay for their glasses.

Contact lenses are as widely worn in Britain as they are in the States, with everything from extended wear to disposable lenses available, but they're incredibly expensive, ranging from £40 on up. Bring extra sets of lenses and glasses with you. Contact solutions are fairly expensive, but not sufficiently so that you should stuff your suitcases with saline. You can buy American products (Lensept, Allergan, and Bausch & Lomb are all here), and there are plenty of European cleaning systems, too. Some students leave their contacts at home and avoid the hassle of heat unit converters and the extra weight in their pack.

You can find an optician in the Yellow Pages, or your GP can recommend someone local.

Family planning. Family planning is well promoted in the U.K., with thousands of clinics providing free counseling and contraceptives throughout the country. Your university health center usually offers some services and, if not, will recommend clinics. A typical visit includes weight and blood pressure checks and, for women, a vaginal examination. Pregnancy tests are also available. Doctors explain each type of contraceptive and how to use it. If they prescribe a contraceptive, they usually ask you to come in for a follow-up visit.

Abortion is legal but is as big an issue in Britain as it is in the States. Less than half of all abortions are done on the NHS which can be "jolly well difficult," especially when some GPs have strong personal feelings against it. An abortion requires permission from two doctors, which further complicates the matter. Even so, your GP is your main source for information and can refer you for further counseling with a hospital consultant. On the NHS, most abortions are carried out by the twelfth or thirteenth week of pregnancy, although the law allows abortions under special circumstances up to the twenty-fourth week. Get advice early if you think you're pregnant, especially if you need NHS care, which always involves a wait.

Private abortion clinics are quicker than the NHS but can be very expensive. Brook Advisory Centers, which cater specifically to young people, are located in major cities and provide counseling and referrals for abortion services. The twenty British Pregnancy Advisory Service Centers offer pregnancy testing, counseling, and advice.

Condoms are more widely available in Britain than in North America, with vending machines in most pubs, clubs, and student union bar bathrooms (both male and female).

AIDS. AIDS information and advice is provided by university health centers and family planning clinics, but it's not always comprehensive. A National AIDS Helpline (0800-567123) is open twenty-four hours a day; there are also local helplines all over Britain. The Terence Higgins Trust, based in London, provides in-depth counseling and legal advice. Sexually Transmitted Disease (STD) Clinics attached to larger hospitals often provide AIDS testing (with counseling before and after the test to explain what your results mean) for a small fee.

Drug abuse. SCODA, the Standing Conference on Drug Abuse, provides a national directory of drug abuse counseling/treatment centers, which offer a range of advice, help and services, usually free. You can get information by calling SCODA at (071) 430-2341.

Homeopathy. The *New World Dictionary* defines homeopathy as "a system of medical treatment based on the theory that certain diseases can be cured by giving very small doses of drugs which in a healthy person and in large doses would produce symptoms like those of the disease." It is treatment with the "hair of the dog that bit you." Homeopaths prescribe small doses of substances that encourage the symptoms of a disease or illness and help your body build its natural resistance.

Although it may sound strange, the concept of homeopathic care has grown recently in the U.K., and even Prince Charles is a devoted fan. There are over six hundred homeopaths throughout the country and five specialized homeopathic hospitals under the NHS. You can see a homeopath for anything you'd go to a regular doctor for (qualified homeopaths are also qualified GPs), from asthma to eczema. The idea is to look at each person as a whole, not at just the symptoms. Homeopathic treatment, however, is not covered by the NHS. Although there are qualified homeopaths working for the NHS, you still have to pay for the treatment.

If you are interested, send a self-addressed, stamped envelope to the British Homeopathic Association for a list of registered homeopaths in your area. In telephone books, homeopathy is lumped under "alternative medicine" with aromatherapy, acupuncture, reflexology, and the like. If you look on your own, make sure that your doctor has the initials MFHOM or FFHOM after his or her name, which indicates official recognition by the Homeopathic Association. Contact the BHA at the following address: 27a Devonshire Street, London W1N 1RJ, United Kingdom; tel. (071) 935-2163.

REPUBLIC OF IRELAND

Ireland has no national health service (although universities generally have health centers on campus), and residents purchase private health care and insurance as in the United States. Carrying personal health insurance while studying in Ireland is a must. If you have Blue Cross/Blue Shield coverage in America, you can shift over to Voluntary Health Insurance (VHI) for one year in Ireland. Contact Blue Cross/Blue Shield at (312) 440-6000 for more information. In Canada, procedures for transferring national health care vary from province to province, so contact your provincial health care authorities for specifics.

Abortion remains illegal in Catholic Ireland (it's legal in Northern Ireland, but only in life-threatening situations), as does telling anyone about where to get one, either in printed documents or as an advisor in a health clinic. Irish women have traditionally traveled to Britain for abortions, where they are permitted up to twenty-four weeks. Irish student unions, led by Trinity College, have fought to make abortion counseling legal. The Trinity Union challenged the law and was taken to the High Court for printing information on counseling in their alternative prospectus.

Contraceptives are also difficult to find, and until 1985 you couldn't purchase them unless you were married. To buy them now you must be over eighteen and visit a chemist. Don't be surprised if they are not prominently displayed at the counter, and in heavily Catholic areas they may not be available at all. The Virgin Record Store in Dublin was legally forced to shut down its short-lived but popular Mates "Condom Counter" by an order of the local magistrates. For information on family planning contact your student union, USI (address in appendix A), or the Irish Family Planning Association,15 Mountjoy Square, Dublin 1, Republic of Ireland; tel. (01) 740723. The latter organization runs two family planning centers in Dublin (59 Synge Street, Dublin 8; tel. (01) 780712/682420; and 5-7 Cathal Brugha Street, Dublin 1; tel. (01) 727363/727276) which dispense advice and contraceptives.

9
Communication

COMMUNICATION BASICS

O nce you arrive in Britain or Ireland, there are some communication differences you will want to master without delay:

☞ **Sign language.** If you make a "V" peace sign with two fingers and turn them around to face someone, you are not ordering two drinks, or two sandwiches, or two anything. You are saying "f— off."

☞ **The toilet.** If you want a bath, you use the bathroom, but if you need the toilet, ask for the toilet, loo, or w.c. (water closet). In less refined company, ask for the bog. In Ireland you'll come across *mná* (women) and *fir* (men), and in Wales *merched* (women) and *dynion* (men).

☞ **Taking the piss.** This is not about toilets but people, and how they get along. In Ireland and Britain it's common for friends and acquaintances alike to take the piss out of you or take the mickey or wind you up. In other words, they'll lie until you buy what they're saying and then laugh at how gullible you are to actually believe them. It's usually done in a friendly spirit and you're welcome to get them back. This happens in North America, too, but it's definitely an art form in Ireland and Britain.

☞ **Bank holiday.** Not just for bankers, a bank holiday is really a national holiday. Everyone gets the day off (except for big city shop assistants, who have to work the cash registers for the inevitable onslaught of holiday shoppers), while the BBC competes with ITV (Independent Television) and Channel 4 to bring you the best TV movies. In smaller towns and cities, nothing opens.

☞ **The first floor.** When you enter most buildings in North America, you're on the first floor, but in Britain and Ireland you're on the ground floor. The first floor is above the ground floor (in North America, the second floor).

☞ **Time.** Timetables for European trains, buses, coaches, and ferries are usually printed in twenty-four-hour military time: 3:30 P.M. becomes 15:30; 12:00 midnight, 24:00.

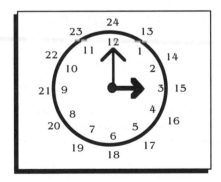

☞ **Dates.** Americans record dates as month/day/year, but the British and Irish use a day/month/year format. Thus April 9, 1991, would be 4/9/91 in Boston, 9/4/91 in Wales.

☞ **Pissed.** This doesn't mean angry (in Britain and Ireland you must be "pissed off"), but mankered, blotto, Brahms and Liszt, rat-arsed, skulled, bevvied, guttered, stotious, steaming, or drunk.

☞ **School, public school, comprehensive school.** In Britain and Ireland, the term school means primary or secondary school, never university or college. A public school is a private school (fancy, expensive ones include Harrow, Howells, Roedean, Gordonstoun (where Prince Charles went), Stowe, Eton, and Bedales), while a comprehensive school is a U.S.-style public (state) school.

☞ **Crisps and chips.** In Britain and Ireland, chips are thick, greasy french fries often covered in salt and vinegar, and crisps are potato chips, often served in little packets at pubs. Flavors include salt and vinegar, and cheese and onion. If you get a craving for pork rinds, try Twiglets.

☞ **Fully licensed versus off-license.** A fully licensed restaurant is licensed to sell alcohol on the premises, while an off-license (or offy) is a liquor store licensed to sell alcohol for consumption off the premises.

☞ **Jiffy, Johnnie, Durex.** This is not peanut butter, your cousin, or Scotch tape (called "Durex" in Australia, a source of confusion for visiting Aussies in stationery stores). They are various names for condoms. However, a rubber is not a condom in Britain or Ireland; it's an eraser.

☞ **Pants.** In Britain and Ireland, pants are underpants, which leads to regular confusion and horror at North American comments like "Oh, gross, I really stained my pants" or "My pants are filthy!"

☞ **Suspenders.** These are not the straps that are an integral part of every investment banker's wardrobe but the far more personal garters (the straps that hold up your stockings). Suspenders are called braces in Britain and Ireland.

☞ **Randy prat.** This is the most embarrassing name to have in Britain or Ireland; randy means horny and prat means jerk. If this is your name, seriously consider studying abroad in Japan.

☞ **Knock up.** If that cute English friend from psych class offers to "knock you up in the morning," don't panic or get too excited. He's only going to knock on your door in order to wake you up (southern England only).

TELEPHONES

Britain

Public *phone boxes* (phone booths) come in a variety of designs and colors. The traditional cast-iron red booth now competes with newer British Telecom (BT) glass models as well as Mercuryphone's Flash Gordon-style entry—blue and silver with peaked tops. Local calls cost 10p, and a small LCD screen tells you how much money you have left (the numbers drop fast on your overseas calls). Two types of BT phonebox exist: those with red or yellow stripes accept coins, while those with green stripes accept only phonecards, which can be purchased at post offices, newsagents, and stores.

Important Numbers

Emergency 999
(police, fire, ambulance)

Operator	**100**
Directory Assistance:	
London	**142**
Elsewhere	**192**
(Including the Republic of Ireland)	
Int'l Operator:	**155**
Int'l Directory Assistance:	**153**

In rural areas, you'll come across the old and adversarial type of British phone box, with no LCD screens to indicate how much money is left and no flexibility when it comes to different types of coin. These are usually black and heavy looking, and require that you dial the number before inserting any money. When the call goes through, you'll hear your party start to answer only to get drowned out by an immediate shower of noisy beeps. Push a 10p coin into the slot and the beeps should quit until your money runs low again. When the beeps resume you have fifteen seconds to drop in another coin.

Ireland

Newer Irish phone boxes look just like those found in Britain. A local call is 20p for five minutes. On most old pay phones, you rest your money in the slot at the top of the phone and dial the number. After the person answers, your money will roll in. Although there are some phone card phones in Ireland, they are few and far between, so it's not worth wasting your money on cards. In general, working pay phones are hard to find in Ireland. During office hours, try the post office.

Important Numbers

Emergency 999
(police, fire, ambulance)

Operator   10

Directory Assistance:
  Ireland: 190
(including Northern Ireland)

Britain   197

Int'l Operator: 114
            (in the Dublin *01* area
            only, otherwise dial **10**)

**Int'l Directory
Assistance: 114**
            (in the Dublin *01* area
            only, otherwise dial **10**)

Local and International Calls

Follow-on calls. In both Ireland and Britain, always press the pay phone button marked *follow-on call* if you want to use any remaining credit for a second call; otherwise, you won't get any change.

Calling within Britain and Ireland. It is most expensive to call long distance within Britain and Ireland from 8:00 A.M. until 1:00 P.M., less expensive to phone between 1:00 P.M. and 6:00 P.M., and cheapest to telephone after 6:00 P.M. and all day Saturday and Sunday.

Calls to Britain and Ireland from North America. British and Irish telephone numbers consist of an area code plus a number. The first digit of the area code is often a zero, but the zero is dropped when you call Britain or Ireland from outside the country.

- *To call Britain from the United States or Canada:*

international code

011 + 44 + area code (minus zero) + number

country code

- *To call Ireland from the United States or Canada:*

international code

011 + 353 + area code (minus zero) + number

country code

- *To call the United States or Canada from Britain:*

country code

010 + 1 + area code + number

international access code

• *To call the United States or Canada from Ireland:*

```
     country code
         |
  16 + 1 + area code + number
  |
 international code
```

It is cheapest to call North America on weekdays between 8:00 P.M. and 8:00 A.M., or anytime on the weekends.

You'll sometimes hear beeps when making international calls from a British or Irish phone box. If you hear beeps when dialing North America, it may be necessary to ask the operator to call you back.

International Collect Calls from Britain and Ireland. To make an international collect call, dial 155 for the international operator in Britain and Northern Ireland, 114 in Dublin, and 10 from everywhere else in the Republic of Ireland. Tell them you want to reverse the charges. The operator will ask you for the number you're calling, the number you're calling from, and your name. In the Republic of Ireland, some operators try to persuade you to make a more expensive person-to-person call by asking for the name of the person you're dialing. If you're not calling anyone in particular, just tell the operator you're phoning home.

Full daytime rates apply for collect calls. It's much cheaper for family and friends to call you, so a good tip is to call home collect, give your number overseas, and wait for them to phone you back. Be aware that charges for collect calls may not appear on your bill back home for up to five months.

Overseas operators: Britain only. You can access an overseas operator from Britain (not from the Republic of Ireland) and thereby avoid the problem of beeps and also use a credit card number. It costs nothing (the same as accessing a British operator). To speak to an operator from home, use the following numbers:

Overseas Operators (Britain only)	
Sprint:	0800-89-0877
AT&T USADirect	0800-89-0011
MCI CALL USA:	0800-89-0222
Canada Direct:	0800-89-0016

POST OFFICE: BRITAIN

Letters: Air Mail

The British postal system is generally reliable, and deliveries are made one or two times a day. First-class letters sent within the country often arrive the next day (but not always), and second-class letters arrive in three. Letters to North America take about one week. They travel faster (as fast as four days to the U.S. east coast) if sent from a large post office, especially one in London. There are separate rates for domestic and European Community service and three air mail zones for mail sent overseas:

Zone A: North Africa, Middle East
Zone B: North and South America (including the U.S. and Canada)
Zone C: Asia (including Australia, New Zealand, and Japan)

There are special rates for small packets, printed papers, and newspapers. Small packets can weigh up to 1 kilogram (kg), must be unsealed (usually tied with string to keep things in), and can contain personal letters. The printed paper rate applies to packages up to 2 kilograms in weight and, like small packets, must be open and tied with string. You can't include personal letters, but you can mail Christmas or other greeting cards at this rate if you don't seal them and don't write more than five words (seriously) in addition to the printed text of the card. You're allowed a signature that won't count in the five-word quota, but remember that the envelope is open for postal employees to check that you didn't go overboard and write six words.

If you send a letter overseas, you have to place a blue airmail sticker in the lower left-hand corner. Stickers are required on postcards as well. Ask for them at the post office.

Surface Mail: Mailing Parcels Home

A package sent from London via surface mail takes up to three months to arrive in North America. This is the most economical way to send home books, papers, and winter clothing once the warmer

months arrive. When packing anything, it's cheaper to send several
small parcels instead of one large box.

Express Mail: Swiftair

The express airmail service in Britain is called Swiftair and operates
through the postal system. Swiftair letters travel by regular mail, but
the Swiftair label guarantees that they're handled before anything
else. Although Swiftair is not as fast as private couriers (Federal
Express, etc.), it's not slow either. Letters from London reach New
York in about three days. Swiftair costs just under £2 in addition to
regular postage, and prepaid swiftpacks are available for items under
60g (grams).

Other British Post Office Services

In addition to mailing letters and parcels, the post office also
handles a huge variety of services and provides forms for many more.
These include *Girobank* (checking and savings accounts, traveler's
checks, cash machines, Visa cards—offices open until 5:30 P.M.);
motor vehicle registration and driver's license application forms;
housing benefit rebates for individuals on welfare; Poll Tax registration forms and pamphlets on how to obtain rebates; and the all-
important TV license application (see page 150).

POST OFFICE: REPUBLIC OF IRELAND

Letters: Air Mail

The Irish post office (An Post) is also reliable, with the best service
available from Dublin. Irish postboxes are, naturally, green. Postcards
and letters conforming to post office preferred (P.O.P.) standards (not
over 20g, about three sheets of A4 or U.S. letter-size paper) cost the
same to send within Ireland or any European Community country.
Heavier letters cost the same to send between Britain and Ireland but
cost more to other EC destinations. Airmail rates for letters sent
outside the EC are uniform.

As in Britain, small packets up to 2kg may be sent at a special rate.
There is also a special airmail rate for printed papers without personal
letters inside. Always write the type of service (e.g., "small packet") on
the outside of the envelope.

Surface Mail: Mailing Parcels Home

As in Britain, a package sent by surface mail (from Dublin) takes up to three months to arrive in North America. This is the most economical way to send home books, papers, and winter clothing once the warmer months arrive.

Express Mail

The Irish post office offers a special overnight National and International Courier Service, which is mainly used for service within Ireland and to Europe, although express service to a few North American destinations is also available. Otherwise, Federal Express is there to get that resumé or transcript home.

10

Sports

FOOTBALL (SOCCER)

Football, known as soccer in America and football just about everywhere else, is the most popular sport in Britain. Teams date from the nineteenth century, when the English and Scottish football associations (FAs) were formed. Today in England there are ninety-six teams in four divisions; each team is ranked, and some twenty or so teams belong in each division. Teams used to belong to divisions because of what region of the country they came from, but they now move from division to division based on promotions and demotions. At the end of each season, the top three teams in a division are promoted to the next higher division, while the bottom three teams are demoted to the next lower division. The worst team is fully ejected from the league to the minors, while the top team in the minors becomes the bottom team in the league. Since major newspapers are based in England, you'll hear a lot about the FA Cup Final, the Superbowl of English football, held each year in May.

The Scots are also avid football fans, with three divisions in their own football association. The premier division has about ten teams and is followed by the first and second divisions, with twelve to fifteen teams each. As in England, there is a system of promotions and demotions and a Scottish FA Cup Final, held at the same time as the English FA Cup on the second Saturday in May. In Scotland, alcohol is banned from the grounds.

British football, and specifically English football, has had a sad and raucous history in recent years. Across much of Europe, English football fans are considered violent and dangerous—"lager louts" or "hooligans" who drink too much and assault those who don't support their team. At Heysel Stadium in Belgium in 1985, Liverpool fans pushed fans of an Italian team against a retaining wall and the wall collapsed, crushing several people. Liverpool was blamed and England banned from international competition for several years. In 1989 almost one hundred fans died in the worst stadium disaster ever, and Liverpool was involved again. At Hillsborough Stadium in Sheffield, supporters crowded through poorly placed turnstiles and were fatally crushed up against another retaining gate. Though some blamed Liverpool fans, it's a point of local pride that they were fully exonerated by an official investigation that placed responsibility for the disaster on outmoded stadium design as well as on the local police, who opened an outer gate, allowing fans to force their way in.

Despite a reputation for violence, English fans point out that they are not alone. Holland and Spain have serious blots on their safety records, too. Football is definitely not a family game. A gang is often associated with each team, and fans of opposing teams are rigorously separated at some matches, relegated to different stands. Leaving the stadium can be a long, organized, almost military operation that involves leading supporters to separate tubes or buses for the ride home.

Nevertheless, football, as the most popular game in Britain, can be a fantastic spectator sport, and without doubt some of your friends will speak about nothing else during the month of May. Call the grounds to reserve seats, and wear the right colors to the match.

NOTE: The citizens of Ashbourne, Derbyshire, play a unique form of the game every Shrove Tuesday (the day before Ash Wednesday) known as the Royal Shrovetide Football Match. Participants brave storms and cold weather to play an eight-hour game, with goal-posts a full three miles apart. The ball weighs about four pounds and rules say it can be kicked, carried, and even buried (a real obstacle considering part of the play takes place in a deep stream). The game pits the Down'ards against the Up'ards. The home team depends on which side of the Henmore Brook one was born on. An eight-hour sequel is played the next day.

CRICKET

Cricket is the second most popular game in Britain and is followed religiously (especially by the English) on Sunday TV and at grounds across the country during the May through September season. Enthusiasm wanes across the borders in Scotland and Wales. Known as a "gentleman's" game, it has little of the violence and hooliganism associated with football. It's a serious sport, the rules are called *laws*, the commentary is arcane and unintelligible, and arguments over procedure can get technical and obscure. Cricket is often compared to baseball, but the only similarity is the use of a bat and ball.

There are four main types of game:

1. Sunday League: one inning per side; forty overs per inning—popular at universities on Sunday afternoons

2. One Day, One Day International: one inning per side; fifty-five overs per inning

3. Ordinary Match: two innings per side; unlimited overs per inning; three days of play

4. Test Match: international games, two innings per side; unlimited overs per inning; up to five days of play

The object of the game is to score more runs during your team's inning than the opposing team scores in theirs. Scoring runs is complex, and any explanation requires a description of the field of play.

The *pitch* or *cricket ground* has a rectangular patch in the center, twenty-two yards long, known as the *wicket*—where much of the action takes place. The term *wicket* also refers to a set of sticks: three thick *stumps* stuck into the ground supporting two thin sticks, or *bails*, laid across the top. The batting team has two batsmen, one at either end of the wicket (area of pitch), who guard the wicket

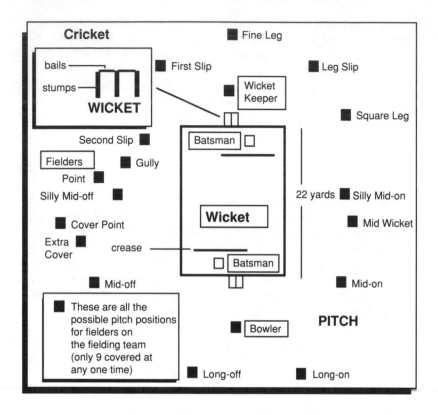

(collection of sticks) by batting away any balls that happen to come their way.

There are two neutral umpires who keep their eye on the game and hand down decisions during play. Each team has eleven men; in the batting team all the players are batsmen. The two "up" batsmen remain on the wicket until they're out, and they're replaced by their teammates according to skill. The first four batsmen are the most experienced on the team; the next four are generally skilled; and the final three aren't renowned for their batting abilities at all. The fielding team also has eleven men, a *bowler* (like a baseball pitcher), a *wicket keeper* (catcher), and nine *fielders,* who stand outside the wicket and chase after batted balls. To sum up:

• *Batting team: eleven batsmen, two up at a time—guard wicket, score runs*

• *Fielding team: nine fielders—try to catch the ball hit by batsman; one wicket keeper—stands behind the wicket; one bowler—tries to hit the opposing team's wicket*

In the standard one-day game, the inning is divided into fifty-five *overs*. An over consists of six pitches (or bowls) by the bowler. The bowler runs forward and tries to hit the wicket with the ball, the batsman tries to bat the ball away, and the fielders, wicket keeper, and bowler all go after the ball.

When the batsman hits the ball, he and the second batsman start running back and forth between the wickets, if they decide that the ball's been hit far or will be difficult to field. As soon as a fielder or the bowler or the wicket keeper retrieves the ball, he'll try throwing it at the wicket, so the batsmen must arrive back at their positions before this happens. Each time the two batsmen cross from one wicket to another is a *run*. If the batsman hits the ball and it bounces out of the pitch, he scores four runs for his team. If the ball goes straight off the pitch without bouncing, six runs are scored.

There are four common ways to get a batsman out:

1. He can be *run out* if a fielder hits the wicket and knocks the bails off while the batter is running.

2. He can be *bowled out* if the bowler gets the ball past the batsman, hits the wicket, and knocks the bails off the stumps.

3. He can be *caught* if the ball is caught in the air without bouncing by the fielders, the bowler, or the wicket keeper.

4. He can be accused of *LBW* (leg before wicket) if the umpire decides that he never attempted to swing at the ball and his leg was blocking the wicket.

The inning in the standard one-day game is finished either after fifty-five overs, or when all the batsmen are out.

Cricket is played in most Commonwealth countries, including India, Australia, New Zealand, and Pakistan. The West Indies team is considered by many to be the best. The English hero has been Ian Botham, the Joe Montana of cricket, most remembered for a match between England and Australia held in Leeds in 1981. England was being annihilated by Australia until Botham ("the Gorilla") started scoring like crazy on the last day, leading his team to victory. You can now see Ian Botham on quiz shows more often than on the pitch. Other noted English batsmen are Alan Lamb, David Gower, and Graham Gooch.

For more information contact the National Cricket Association at Lords Cricket Ground, St. John's Wood Road, London NW8; tel. (081) 286-8011. Other major cricket grounds that host test matches include Old Trafford (Manchester), Edgbaston (Birmingham), Headlingley (Leeds), and The Oval (London).

RUGBY

A padless forerunner of American football, rugby is a popular game in Britain and Ireland, especially in South Wales and the Borders near Scotland. There are two televised forms of the sport, Rugby Union, an amateur sport with fifteen players on each team, and Rugby League, the professional game with thirteen players per side and slightly different rules. Rugby League is more common in the north of England, but hallowed grounds for Union are at Twickenham, in southwest London, and Cardiff Arms Park near the University of Wales, College Cardiff.

The object of rugby is to score as many *tries* (goals worth four points) as possible during the eighty minutes of play. A try is awarded when a player touches the ball (shaped like a large football) to the ground in the opponent's *try zone* (much like American football's *end zone*, an area at each end of the field behind the *try line*). Following a try, the scoring team can attempt a *conversion* (kicking the ball through the goalposts) for two more points.

Play begins when the ball is kicked forward a minimum of ten yards toward the opposing team. Whichever team recovers the ball either kicks or carries it forward (toward their opponent's try zone) or passes laterally or slightly backward (forward passes are illegal) so it can be carried forward by a teammate. The opposing team can only tackle the player with the ball, who must either pass the ball backward to a teammate or release the ball upon hitting the ground. Once the ball is free, either team may recover possession and proceed toward the opponent's try zone.

Play is suspended if the ball goes out of bounds or if an infringement is committed. Infringements can be serious breaches of game regulations, like a high tackle (grabbing someone around the neck), or less serious, like a forward pass or a *knock-on* (when a player throws or knocks the ball forward, intentionally or unintentionally). If a serious infringement is called against a team, they must retreat ten meters back and cannot advance until the ball is back in play. The other team is awarded a penalty, at which point they can *kick for post* (attempt to kick it through the goalposts from wherever they are on the pitch for three points), or run a prearranged play to advance the ball.

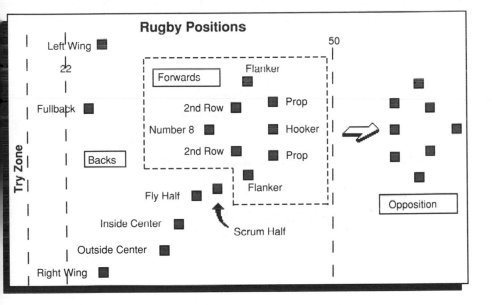

The team is divided into eight *forwards* and seven *backs;* all players are both offensive and defensive. The forwards, also known as the *pack* or the *scrum*, tend to be the larger players and do the majority of the tackling. The backs are the faster runners; the scrum tries to get the ball to the backs whenever possible so that they can run it forward.

There are some basic terms it will help to be familiar with. A minor infringement results in an organized *scrumdown,* during which the forwards of each team face each other and arrange themselves in a tightly linked huddle, with each pack pushing forward against the other. The ball is inserted into the middle of the huddle, and each pack tries to *ruck* over it (push forward so that the ball ends up behind them and accessible to the rest of their team). A *maul* occurs when teams fight for the ball by passing it hand-to-hand, while a ruck involves fighting for control of the ball with the feet. When the ball goes out of play along a sideline, a *line out* results, which is similar to a jump ball in basketball but includes some or all of the pack, lined in single file opposite matching players in the opposing pack.

Many nations play rugby, and the All Blacks (New Zealand), Springboks (South Africa), and Wallabees (Australia) are all considered to be excellent teams. The big rugby events in Britain and Ireland are the International Matches played in February and March, involving teams from England, Scotland, Wales, Ireland, and France. Among the home nations (England, Scotland, Wales, and Ireland), if one wins against the other three they've won the triple crown. If they beat France, too, it's a grand slam. The Scotland/England match, fiercely contested and charged with nationalist overtones, is called the Calcutta Cup. The World Cup, involving teams from around the globe, is held every four years in a participating country.

For more information on rugby, contact *Rugby Magazine*, The Rugby Press Ltd., 2530 Broadway, New York, N.Y. 10024; tel. (212) 787-1160.

HURLING (CAMOGIE) AND GAELIC FOOTBALL

Like much of Irish culture, the game of hurling (camogie is the women's version) is rooted in legend and nationalism. It supposedly began when the legendary hero, Chuculainn, killed a hound by batting a stone into its mouth. In 1884 the Gaelic Athletic Association (GAA) was founded, drawing up both hurling and Gaelic football rules and forming the leagues to play in. During the Great Famine, the British prevented the Irish from playing soccer with local British garrisons (the best teams at the time with access to high-quality equipment), and hurling became the highly popular and nationalist alternative. At Irish universities it's as familiar and widespread as rugby.

Hurling, similar to field hockey, is played on a field 145 meters long and 90 meters wide. Each team has fifteen players, including the goalie (although there are only nine on the field at any given time). Each player holds a *hurley,* a long ash stick (like a hockey stick) used to hit the ball *(sliodor)* between the opponent's goalposts. Games are divided into two 30-minute halves (senior intercounty championship halves are 35 minutes).

An umpire stands by each of the four goalposts and determines if a team has scored a point. These are recorded by tossed flags— a green flag when someone makes a goal (worth three points). There are two linesmen, one on each side, to determine who gets

Hurling

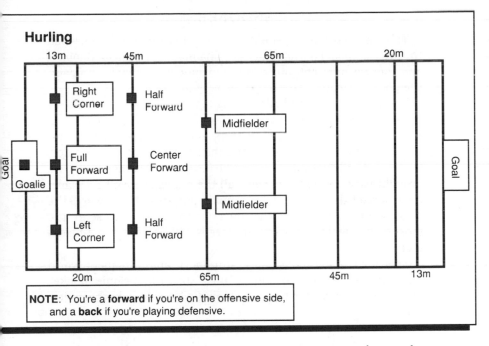

NOTE: You're a **forward** if you're on the offensive side, and a **back** if you're playing defensive.

possession if the ball goes out. There is just one referee, who follows all play and makes all final calls. His call takes precedence over the calls of other officials.

To begin the game, the referee rolls the sliodor between the midfielders, who wildly attack it with their hurleys. Once a team gains possession of the sliodor, they can balance it at the end of the hurley (not an easy task) or *hop it* (bounce it at the end of the hurley) down the field. Whether hopping or balancing, these are called *solo runs*.

You can carry the sliodor without the hurley if you have a *clash of the ash*—when you hit another hurley, breaking yours or knocking it out of your hands. If this happens, you carry the ball, dropping and kicking it every three steps.

Gaelic football is another native Irish sport. It uses the same field, player positions, and point system as hurling. However, it uses a different ball (more like a soccer ball) and there's no hurley. You can use your hands to carry the ball down the field, although you must drop and kick the ball every three steps.

For more information on hurling, camogie, and Gaelic football (including specific rules), contact the Gaelic Athletic Association, Croke Park, Dublin 3, Republic of Ireland; tel. (01) 363222.

SNOOKER

Televised and popular, snooker comes alive in the autumn, when the international Pool and Snooker Championship is held. Snooker and pool are different, but related: in snooker the table is bigger, the pockets smaller, and the rules very different.

There are fifteen red balls on the table, plus the *colors,* one of each with differing point values: yellow (two points), green (three), brown (four), blue (five), pink (six), and black (seven). You first sink a red ball (worth one point), then follow it up with a color. Once a red ball goes into a pocket, it stays, but the other colors are brought back on the table. Once all the red balls are off the table, the colored balls are sunk in order of importance (black, worth the most points, is the last). The object of the game is to score the most points, and the maximum score is 147 (red-black-red-black-etc).

Snooker is a big-money spectator sport, and a frequent world champion is Britain's "Mr. Interesting," Steve Davis. Some snooker players wear incredibly bizarre, sloping glasses to help them view the table.

GOLF

Golf began in Scotland at the hallowed St. Andrews course, invented by the Royal and Ancient Golf Club in 1754. While English, Welsh, and Irish courses are privately owned, many Scottish golf courses are run by municipalities and are open to the public for a small fee. If you are a student at the University of St. Andrews, you're entitled to become a member of the club for about £45 a year, giving you access to all four club courses, including the Old Course, where the game began.

For more information on golf, contact the Royal and Ancient Golf Club of St. Andrews, Fife KY16 9JD, Scotland; tel. (0334) 72112.

DARTS

There is reason to question the sanity of people who mix alcohol with pointy little spears thrown at a board (often right by the toilet, where customers pass preoccupied with concerns of their own), but darts in the pub is a time-honored British/Irish tradition. If you want to play, the pubkeep will hand over three darts per player for a small fee (usually just a deposit).

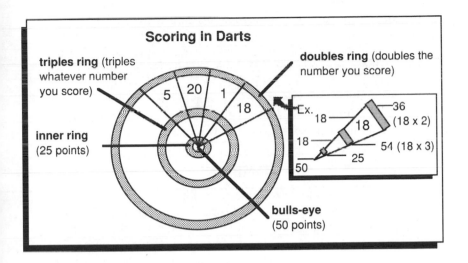

Scoring in Darts

Weapons in hand, there are many games to play. The most popular are these:

☞ **501 Down.** This is the standard professional darts game. The number one player in Britain is Eric Bristow, known as the "Crafty Cockney." You start with 501 points and subtract the value of every shot until you reach zero. The minimum number of darts needed to win is nine (eight triple 20s and a triple seven), but this feat has only been accomplished once on TV by John Lowe, earning him a £100,000 bonus (think how badly your hand would shake). The last shot must bring you exactly to zero, or else you go *bust* (lose your turn).

☞ **Cricket.** There are as many variations to this game as there are rules to the real game of cricket. In one variation, one player is the *bowler* and the other is the *batsman* (or *batswoman*). They throw alternately, the bowler trying to hit the batsman's *wicket* six times (inner ring = one wicket; bull's-eye = two wickets). The batsman goes first and must score a minimum of forty points before scoring any runs (e.g., forty=no runs, forty-one=one run). Once the batsman is out (when six wickets are scored by the bowler), the players swap positions for a second *inning* of the game.

☞ **Killer.** This game begins by tossing a dart with your least-skilled hand (e.g., if you're right-handed, use your left) to choose your *number* for the game (whatever number your dart lands on). For the rest of the game, you can only score points by hitting your own number. If you hit it three times, you become a *killer* and can start hitting numbers belonging to your opponents. When you hit an opponent's number, you subtract those points from the opponent's score; a player whose score drops below zero is *dead* (loses the game).

GAMBLING

Betting on everything from American football to whether snow will fall on Christmas is legal and widely practiced in Britain and Ireland, with shops paying up to £1,000,000 per bet. You'd have to bet high and be extraordinarily lucky to come anywhere close to such winnings, but since wagers of 10p are accepted, you don't need to sell the farm to enjoy Mecca, Ladbroke's, William Hill's, or any other betting shops across the islands.

Betting shops in some areas are run-down, all-male enclaves, but the newer ones on major streets are hi-tech operations, with racy interiors, coffee bars, and walls of video screens revealing the latest scores. Odds on most gambling sports (horses, greyhound racing, soccer) are posted, and others (American football) can be requested. When placing your bet (the money you put down is called the *stake*), make sure you pay the 10 percent tax. Otherwise you'll be taxed on your winnings.

A single bet is a bet on one event; for example, that Horse #6 will come in first. A double bet is a bet on two events; for example, that Horse #6 will come in first and Horse #4 will place second. Along these lines, a triple bet is a bet on three separate events, and anything higher is called an accumulator bet. An each-way bet is a bet that your horse (or greyhound, or team) will come in first or will place (come in second or third). Each-way bets cost twice as much as a single bet, but there's a greater chance of return on your wager (the return on the place bet is the smaller).

Pubs throughout Britain are inundated by flashy, tacky, noisy electronic slot machines known as *fruit machines,* so called because they once masqueraded as clever hi-tech ads for fruit-flavored chewing gum back in the 1950s when all gambling mechanisms were illegal. Students advise that you wait for someone else to spend all his or her money in a machine without winning before emptying your own wallet (although there's no real reason why you'd then have a better chance; the odds just seem better).

In Ireland, the national lottery *(Lotto)* costs 50p a game, although you must buy two games at a time for IR£1. Pick the right six numbers and you could be flying home first class. There's also a special Dublin-based lottery, where the money goes both to winnings and to help the handicapped.

11

Entertainment and the Media

No doubt you'll get pretty tired of the four walls of your flat or room while keeping your nose to the grindstone. When you do, there are plenty of things to do. In London the best guides to what's happening around town are *Time Out* and *City Limits* magazines. Both sell for a little over a pound and are filled with theater, cinema, comedy, cabaret, and television listings. Free sources of information are the widely available Australasian magazines *Southern Cross, TNT,* and *LAW.* Grab them outside any tube station.

For entertainment and events in Edinburgh and Glasgow, get your copy of *The List* for about 90p at most newsagents and bookstores. In the Welsh capital of Cardiff, pick up *What's Happening* for about £1, or a free *Events in Cardiff* from the tourist office. In Belfast, you can pick up *What's On* at the tourist office or check the listings in the *Belfast Telegraph.* In Dublin, look for the easy-to-remember *In Dublin,* available for about IR£1. There's also the free *Dublin Event Guide,* available everywhere (the tourist office, restaurants, Kinlay House, USIT, etc).

THEATER

British theater is about the best in the world, and the opportunity to see great performances unmatched. And it's not outrageously expensive. Peter O'Toole, Julie Walters, new plays and Shakespeare make for live entertainment like nowhere else. Small cities sport local companies, major productions travel, and the sheer number of London shows (big name and fringe) is phenomenal. Plus, there are plenty of drama groups on most campuses for anyone interested in taking part. West End shows are big productions performed in the West End area of London, where the major theaters are located. With a student card, the cost of a West End show is £5-£20 (fringe shows even less). It can be cheaper to see a play than a film. The best tickets are student standby tickets (or concessions) available at the theater an hour or so before each performance; join the queue. You can also queue up for return tickets (or returns), tickets cancelled the day of the performance. Get to the theater several hours early to purchase returns for popular plays. Steer well clear of ticket agents, who charge outrageous commissions, and *ticket touts* (or scalpers) who are master rip-off artists. In London, half-price tickets can be bought at the Leicester Square Ticket Booth (run by SWET, the Society of West End Theatre), but they're sometimes expensive seats to begin with so the discount only helps you a bit (their prices are better on the longer-running shows such as *The Phantom of the Opera* or *Les Miserables*).

When you buy your ticket, there are a few terms that may throw you. *Stalls* are orchestra seats, *circle* the first balcony, and *upper circle* the upper balcony. Actors often aim their performance for the circle (first balcony), so these seats can be very good. While the upper balcony is most popular with budget-conscious students, some theaters have such stratospheric upper circles (also known, for good reason, as *the Gods)* that you'll need oxygen and climbing gear. Small red binoculars help in these conditions. They're fastened to the seat backs and cost only 20p to rent.

London is not the only place to experience theater in Britain; several internationally renowned companies operate outside the city. The Edinburgh International Festival offers spectacular theater, as well as music, art showings, and general cultural mayhem for three crazy weeks in August. Glasgow's Mayfest (or International Festival of Arts) is one of the most wide-ranging arts festivals in Europe and runs the first two weeks of May. The Welsh National Eisteddfod, a week-long festival celebrating Welsh traditions of storytelling and song, is held alternately in the north and south of Wales each August. The Royal Exchange in Manchester, the Playhouse and Everyman theaters in Liverpool, the Royal Shakespeare Theatre in Stratford-upon-Avon, the Phoenix in Leicester, the Old Vic in Bristol, and many more provide top-quality performances in other parts of the Kingdom.

The Abbey in Dublin is the national theater of Ireland, founded in 1904 by William Butler Yeats. While it once shocked audiences with a scandalous production of "Playboy of the Western World," recent plays have been more mainstream. Still, theater, from Shakespeare to experimental, thrives in the Green Isle, mostly in Dublin or at the Opera House in Cork.

CINEMA

Get it right: the *theater* is where plays are performed and the *cinema* is where you go to see a *film*. Saying "movie" in Britain or Ireland is sometimes considered pretentious (like saying "I'm going to a film" in the States). Films are as expensive in London as in New York and L.A., but discounts are often available on Mondays. The price in outlying areas is about £3, and university film societies are even cheaper. Britain and Ireland have fewer cinemas (and fewer multiplexes) than you find in North America. You might want to resist going to the movies before heading overseas because these same films will play in Britain and Ireland a few months later and you'll end up seeing everything for the second time.

The British scoff at the advertisements on American television, and save their own ads for the cinema. Before the start of each film, along with previews and warnings on trash and smoking, come anywhere from ten to forty-five minutes of commercials. Most are enjoyable, but if you prefer, you can skip them; some cinemas post separate times for the adverts and film.

TELEVISION

Britain

If there's one topic that causes more debate between U.S. and British students than anything else, it's the telly. The British are fiercely proud of the BBC, which controls two of their four available channels (a fifth television channel, the third commercial channel, is planned for the early 1990s), and signs off each night about 1:00 A.M.

No advertisements are allowed (except endless promotions for BBC shows), but people pay for this privilege. Those owning TVs support the network by purchasing an annual television license, currently over £70 for a color set. To enforce payment, TV police drive about in hi-tech vans able to determine exactly when and where a television is operating and whether it is properly licensed. If not, they can enter your home.

"The BBC aims to entertain and inform," British students will explain smugly, "while that American crap of yours simply entertains." This is the McDonald's phenomenon, where the British loudly decry the symbolism but scarf down the food itself. There is at least one American show per night on the two independent networks, which sport so many commercials and U.S. copies like "Blind Date" ("Dating Game"), "Kilroy" ("Donahue" on Valium), and the morning news and entertainment program, "Good Morning Britain", that they're indistinguishable from ABC, NBC, and CBS. American programs return the favor by copying British shows. "Three's Company" was from "Man about the House" and "Dear John" comes, simply enough, from "Dear John." Ancient U.S. shows like "The Waltons" are popular in Britain, and there's even a "Wheel of Fortune," with a British Vanna turning the letters on command.

British advertisements differ from American commercials in that they're not as shamelessly blunt and don't hit you over the head with their message. "Hemorrhoids? Try soothing relief with Anusol" or "Mom, do you douche with Eve?" just wouldn't play well in the Kingdom. British adverts are more subtle, sometimes making the viewer wait until the end to reveal what they're trying to sell.

British TV produces some excellent shows. "Spitting Image" is the finest in rude political satire, and uses grossly caricatured puppets that drool and spit to make their point. "Blue Peter," a wholesome magazine program covering current affairs, arts, and drama, is the classic children's television program that adults also like to watch, while Barry Norman provides more laid-back film reviews than Siskel and Ebert. Long nature shows are standard BBC offerings, and you can spend a quiet afternoon learning about the "Life of the Burrowing Red-Bummed Vole." Investigative reporting is top-notch. An independent news show uncovered the evidence that reopened the case of the Guildford Four, Irish nationals wrongly jailed for fifteen years for allegedly planting bombs in Surrey pubs. In general, British news programs are so far ahead of ratings-conscious U.S. commercial attempts (PBS offerings are notable exceptions) that many Americans

feel incredibly embarrassed. The rest of British TV provokes significantly less envy among American students, especially sitcoms, which
even some British admit are superior in the States (note the long-
running, popular U.K. success of "Cheers").

ITV (Independent Television) is the only station that varies in
different regions of the country, giving local programming a chance.
Channel 4 (C4) is a nationwide commercial station known for its
popular offbeat offerings.

The most popular shows in Britain are the soap operas.
"Eastenders" follows residents of London's Cockney East End, "Coro-
nation Street" covers a working-class community in Lancashire, and
"Brookside" is about a Liverpool housing estate. British soaps are a bit
dreary but less glitzy and more realistic than their American cousins.
Still, hands-down, the worst soaps are neither British nor American,
but Australian. "Neighbours," which once starred pop idols Kylie
Minogue and Jason Donovan, is both atrocious and vastly popular.
Trivia books, fan clubs, and regular schlock features in the tabloids
attest to its huge following. Few claim that this show, or other Aussie
imports like "Home and Away," are really meant to inform.

British Sky Broadcasting (B Sky B) is Rupert Murdoch's satellite TV
system, offering the nation's viewers a choice of at least four channels, more if they purchase a satellite dish. Everything from MTV to
laugh-tracked, sitcom-saturated U.S. programming is there for the
viewing.

Daily television listings are printed in most newspapers, while *Time
Out* magazine provides a comprehensive schedule of offerings for each
week. The *TV Times* covers only Channel 4 and ITV, and the *Radio
Times,* BBC1 and BBC2.

Ireland

Irish television also requires an annual license, and the main
channels are Radio Telefis Éireann 1 (RTE1) and Network 2. Radio
Telefis Éireann is the government-run, BBC-type station, offering
Irish cultural programs and recapping the daily news in Irish
Gaeilge. Channel 2 (or Network 2) is the main commercial station,
offering popular shows like "Please Please Please Me," which inves-
tigates humorous aspects of the modern Irish marriage. Many
Irish have piped TV (or pTV, cable television) that gives them
access to the British stations BBC1, BBC2, and Channel 4 plus, in
certain regions, the independent U.K. stations UTV (Ulster Televi-

sion, from Northern Ireland), HTV (Harlech TV, from Wales), and S4C (Sianel 4 Cymru, also Welsh). Popular Irish programs include U.S. imports, "Dublin Fair City" (a soap opera set around a community center and, naturally, a pub), and the afternoon show "Zig & Zag," featuring puppet characters popular with both kids and adults.

NOTE: One area where both British and Irish news reporting suffers is in their coverage of the situation in Northern Ireland. In both countries, interviews with the IRA are banned, and while reporters can report what members of Sinn Féin (the political arm of the IRA) say, they can't play voice or video recordings. This is known as *Section 42* in the Republic of Ireland, a broadcasting ban on anyone supporting violence. Only a fraction of Northern Ireland's daily struggle is shown on TV. In Britain, a storm of controversy began in 1988, when police raided the offices of the BBC in Scotland, confiscating videotapes relating to events in Northern Ireland.

VIDEOTAPES

Videotapes from North America will not work on videocassette recorders in Britain or Ireland unless the recorder is equipped with a special *NTSC/PAL* switch that allows it to accept both formats. Tapes recorded at home can also be converted at selected video stores, but this is expensive.

NEWSPAPERS

Britain

The British Press was once based in Fleet Street in London, but offices are now scattered about the capital. Several papers also operate on the Isle of Dogs in the Docklands area. Because television programming is limited and doesn't dominate the culture as it does in North America, more people turn to papers for news and information. British papers are substantial but don't kill as many trees as those in the States. Nothing approaches the size, variety, content, or advertising of a U.S. big-city Sunday edition. Newspapers are generally either dailies (printed Monday through Friday or Saturday) or Sunday editions only. It's important to note that some British papers editorialize openly in their news articles and have distinct political slants. This makes them a lot more interesting than many bland American offerings, but be aware of what you're reading. Buy your newspaper at a newsagent, who'll likely offer a selection of cards, stationery, magazines, and candy along with the daily rags. Some of the most well-known newspapers are the following:

☞ **The *Independent.*** Probably the most moderate and complete daily paper, with solid investigative reporting and a good balance of foreign and domestic news. It also focuses a bit on business to appeal to readers in the "City," London's financial district. Some find it so moderate, complete, and appealing to City readers that it's boring. On Saturdays, the *Independent Magazine* is well known and applauded for its excellent photographs. The *Independent on Sunday* has an insightful arts magazine.

☞ **The *Guardian.*** Originally based in Manchester, this paper leans to the left. It puts an emphasis on the arts and social issues and includes a second section that deals with education, health, entertainment, and other areas in turn throughout the week, with a corresponding jobs list at the end of each section. It also offers one of the few women's pages. The *Guardian* is the only quality paper run by an editorial board and not by a single owner. It thus claims to be the most independent newspaper in the country. It used to be called the *Grauniad* because of spelling errors, but since shifting to computerized printing, style and accuracy have vastly improved.

☞ **The *Daily Telegraph.*** Known as the *Torygraph* because of its lean to the right. Supposedly the best financial section. Read by pensioners and World War II veterans. Also popular with Canadian students because Conrad Black, the publisher, is a Canadian with an interest in ice hockey: "The *Telegraph's* the only paper with any Canadian sports news." The *Telegraph* has taken over as the paper of record from the declining *Times.*

☞ **The *Times.*** Once a well-respected chronicler of the national experience, its image is now tarnished from being taken over by media mogul Rupert Murdoch (who, by the way, recently endowed a Chair in Language and Communications at prestigious Oxford University). Considered right-wing. The *Sunday Times* is a better respected, thick, news-packed paper with a book review. The *Times*

Higher Education Supplement (THES) is a separate paper that comes out Fridays, containing news on universities and polytechnics and an extensive listing of job offerings in higher education (similar to the *Chronicle of Higher Education* published in the U.S.).

☞ **The *Observer*.** Publishes a Sunday paper and Sunday magazine. Respected and moderate-to-left, with a regular column covering American topics. Faced with a barrage of new competitive upstarts (e.g., the *Independent on Sunday)*, this paper likes to point out that "it wasn't born yesterday" (founded 1791). Good review section.

☞ **The *Financial Times (FT)*.** A pink (some claim peach, or Necco-wafer orange) *Wall Street Journal* reporting on money matters and the City. Also has excellent Latin American coverage, plus rare, in-depth analyses of U.S./U.K. relations and the European Community.

☞ **The *Evening Standard, Leader, Herald,* etc.** Evening edition papers that come out after 12:00 noon. Major cities have them, and they are the best source of information on finding flats (call immediately from the first edition; flats go fast), mopeds, used furniture, bicycles, or anything else you might be after. Liverpool has the *Echo,* Brighton the *Argus,* etc. London's is the *Standard,* the only paper still printing *six* editions per day.

☞ **The *Scotsman*.** A well-respected, moderate, Edinburgh-based daily paper. Known as "Scotland's National Newspaper."

☞ **The *Sun*.** Another Murdoch entry, infamous for its bare-chested page three Girls (occasionally supplemented by page seven Guys). A right-wing tabloid in line with the *New York Post,* the *Sun* regularly assaults the nation's intelligence but remains avidly read by a large group of fans. Plenty of horoscopes, diet tips, sexist columns, news of the Royals, and photographs. Similar papers include the *Star, Today,* and *News of the World.* The *Daily Mail* is another tabloid, considered "bad, but not that bad."

☞ **The *Daily Mirror*.** The only left-leaning tabloid put out by rival mogul, the late Robert Maxwell. The *Daily Record* is the Maxwell entry in Scotland. Color, sex, violence, the works.

☞ **The *Sunday Sport*.** "Overweight Wife Flattens Hubby in Fan Dance!" "Woman Gives Birth to Child Cannibal!" "Girl Tortured by Blender—and Lives!" The *National Enquirer* for the other side of the Atlantic.

Ireland

In Ireland you have a choice of most British and local Irish papers, although British papers are cheaper, because of a tax on Irish publications. Buy Irish papers at university student unions to avoid this tax. Ireland still has, to a degree, a *unionist* (in favor of Northern Ireland remaining part of the U.K.) versus *nationalist* (Catholic, favoring Northern Ireland becoming part of the Irish Republic) split among newspapers. "Irish papers continue to take sides drawn from memories of the Anglo-Irish War (1919-1921)," claim several Irish students in the Republic. Among your options:

☞ **The *Irish Independent*.** Considered a nationalist-leaning, slightly conservative newspaper that "endorses the values of Catholicism and the State." Seen as lighter and less wordy than the *Irish Times*.

☞ **The *Irish Times*.** Originally a Protestant, pro-U.K. newspaper, the *Times* is more unionist and is considered the best of the national papers by many students. It is described as "socially conscious and bourgeois; very middle of the road," and it boasts a daily supplement section covering, for example, Property, Weekend, and Working and Living (jobs, careers, education).

☞ **The *Irish Press*.** A nationalist paper founded by the political party Fianna Fáil. Considered "less party-oriented but still very much theirs."

☞ **The *Republican News*.** Put out by Sinn Féin. The *News* is available at Sinn Féin offices in Belfast and Dublin and in many republican pubs. Considered "strongly nationalist."

NOTE: Both *USA Today* and the *International Herald Tribune* are available in major British and Irish cities. The *Tribune* contains articles, columns, and editorials excerpted from the *Washington Post* and the *New York Times*. The *Wall Street Journal* is also available in Britain and Ireland.

BRITISH/IRISH
SUBVERSIVE PUBLICATIONS

In Britain pick up *Private Eye* for hilarious and pointed attacks on the government, or *Viz* for gut-level humor (characters like the "Fat Slags" grace its pages). The *Phoenix* is Ireland's version of *Private Eye*, while *Hot Press* is a popular music magazine with interviews and a "healthy focus on alternative politics."

RADIO

Britain

British radio was once tightly controlled in an effort to keep a balance between entertainment and information, like British TV. In other words, there was limited choice. The government recently relaxed radio restrictions and opened up more frequencies for purchase by local stations; consequently, the variety is increasing. Most cities have a local BBC station, which generally plays pop music and gives away free trips if you wear the right T-shirt or paste the right bumper sticker on your car. Four national BBC stations are accessible across the country (a fifth station is slated for airing in the next few years). These four stations are very different from one another, ranging from stereotypical pop with annoying DJs and nonstop giveaways to muzak to high-quality classical cuts to news and current events. Some bigger cities sport independent stations, mostly pop music, like Capital Radio in London. University stations on campus let students try their hand as DJs, hosts, and newsreaders, while pirate radio stations broadcast from Europe or ships in the North Sea. Ask students for the best of these.

Radio Times magazine, available at newsagents, provides scheduling information for Radio One, Two, Three, and Four (as well as BBC1 and BBC2 on telly).

Ireland

RTE1 is the government station, offering regular news reports and cultural programs. Gay Borne is a well-known talk show host who reviews books, films, and current events. Two FM is a popular pop/rock station now forced by the government to broadcast more public service programs. Gerry Ryan is Two's answer to Gay Borne, with a show aimed at young people. FM 3 is Ireland's classical music station. Commercial stations like Century (100FM Dublin, 101FM in Limerick, Cork) and Capital 104 offer music along with plenty of talk, phone-ins and discussion (commercial radio is required to broadcast news 20 percent of the time). Raidío Na Gaeltachta, heard mostly in the Irish-speaking west (Connemara, Tir Chonaill, Corca Dhuibhne), broadcasts news, music, and cultural programs in the Irish language. All four BBC stations are also heard throughout the Republic of Ireland.

SHOPPING

Food Stores

In many parts of Britain and Ireland, small shops are the norm; you'll buy your fruits and vegetables at the local grocery, meat at the butcher (or *victuallers* in Ireland), and bread at the bakery. Never touch fruit in a small grocery; they have a limited stock and don't want you bruising it, so they'll choose your apple or banana for you. There are large food stores (predominantly in Britain), but they're generally smaller with fewer products and brand names than North American supermarkets. Don't expect five different kinds of oat bran on the shelves; no aisles full of over-the-counter drugs either. For cold remedies, aspirin, and the British J. Collis Brown's mixture (a potent stomach-calming hangover remedy with morphine and chloroform which is available over the counter), go to the chemist.

You will have a difficult time locating some American standards such as Pop Tarts, tortillas, and Oreo cookies. Some products are available in special London stores like Harrods or Fortnum and Mason, some in your local Safeway; and small delis throughout the country carry eclectic selections of North American foods, depending on what the owner cares to stock.

☞ **Sainsbury's.** More prevalent down south; relatively cheap and large supermarket; sells sweet potatoes; stocks Old El Paso nachos and taco fixings; popular with students.

☞ **ASDA.** A new breed of supermarket (which the British term a *hypermarket)* that is larger and more spacious than older stores. The bigger ones sell clothes and houseplants in addition to food.

☞ **Marks and Spencers.** Somewhat expensive but high-quality food with the St. Michael's label; few loose fruits (mostly bags of eight, packets of six); very clean with everything wrapped in plastic. Sells a wide range of "idiot-proof," precooked, single-person meals.

☞ **Tesco.** Ordinary supermarket; good vegetables, greens section; trying hard to become "Britain's greenest grocer" with a line of environmentally friendly products.

BOOKSTORES

Britain

British bookstore chains are miles ahead of their North American counterparts like Barnes & Noble, B. Daltons, Waldenbooks, or Crown. Aside from WH Smith, they all offer extensive selections in pleasant surroundings. In London the best area for stores selling new and used books is Charing Cross Road. Small stores along the narrow streets leading off it (try Cecil's Court) offer interesting and eclectic selections. Take the tube to Leicester Square or Tottenham Court Road. However, the "book capital" is not London but tiny Hay-on-Wye, on the Welsh border with England, boasting an annual international literary festival each May, plus miles of secondhand shops.

British paperbacks are expensive, generally around £4-7 each, but at least there's no sales tax, or what the British call *VAT (value-added tax)*.

☞ **Waterstones.** Offers an excellent selection (especially travel books) in an enjoyable atmosphere. "They'll order anything for you (including hard-to-find items from reading lists)," according to students. In Ireland, Waterstones has stores in both Dublin and Cork.

☞ **Sherratt & Hughes.** Smaller than Waterstones; good selection; found on many university campuses.

☞ **Dillon's** (82 Gower Street, London WC1E 6EQ; tel. (071) 636-1577, tube: Goodge Street). Very wide range of titles; huge store across from ULU, the University of London (student) Union.

☞ **James Thin Booksellers.** A popular campus bookstore at Scottish universities, and especially good for academic titles and texts.

☞ **Hatchard's** (187 Piccadilly, London W1A 1ER; tel. (071) 437-3924, tube: Green Park). Terrific selection; their main store along Piccadilly is the oldest bookshop in London (established in 1797).

☞ **Foyles** (119 Charing Cross Road, London WC2; tel. (071) 437-5660, tube: Tottenham Court Road). A one-of-a-kind bookstore in London along Charing Cross Road; "the British version of the Strand (New York), or Powell's (Portland, OR)." Offers a huge selection of titles. Totally disorganized and the staff doesn't know where anything is, but "great for browsing."

☞ **Collet's** (129-131 Charing Cross Road, London WC2H; tel. (071) 734-0782/3, tube: Tottenham Court Road). Chain store specializing in drama, fiction, politics, social sciences, trade unions, and the peace movement; books, bumper stickers, buttons, T-shirts, cards, and posters.

☞ **Orbis Books** (66 Kenway Road, London SW5 0RD; tel. (071) 370-2210, tube: Earl's Court). London bookstore specializing in East European titles: books in Czech, Polish, Hungarian, Russian, and English translations. If they don't have a book in stock, they'll refer you to Book Export, at 206 Blythe Road ((071) 602-5541).

☞ **Neal Street East** (5 Neal Street, London WC2H 9PU; tel. (071) 240-0135, tube: Covent Garden). London bookstore specializing in Far East titles, crafts, and cards.

☞ **WH Smith.** The Waldenbooks of Britain: pulp novels, high sale, mass audience titles; small selection; sells magazines, newspapers, stationery, and candy; in every railway station in Britain.

Ireland

As might be expected, considering its literary history, Ireland is loaded with books—specialty stores, new and used selections. But watch out for the prices; paperbacks are outrageously expensive (IR£6-£9 with a hefty sales tax) in the Republic of Ireland.

☞ **Hodges Figgis** (57/58 Dawson Street, Dublin 2; tel. (01) 774754). The premier shop for Irish literature, history, politics, Celtic Studies, and books in the Irish language; plus travel, fiction, poetry, drama.

☞ **Easons** (40/42 Lower O'Connell Street, Dublin 2). Plenty of Irish tales, stories, poetry, Irish political books on the ground floor; stationery, pens, thumbtacks, photo frames upstairs; has good selection of newspapers from around the country; stores in Cork, Galway.

☞ **Fred Hanna's** (27 Nassau Street, Dublin 2). Across from Trinity College, this is a popular store with students. New books, old books, used books, collector's items, the works.

NOTE: Check out the special sections on local/native writers at bookstores (even the chains), especially in Scotland, Wales, and Ireland.

RECORD STORES

Records and tapes are about £6-£8 each, and CDs run higher at £9-£12. CDs, records, and tapes are each a few pounds more in Ireland.

☞ **HMV.** From His Master's Voice; boasts the largest store in Britain on Oxford Street.

☞ **Our Price.** The British Sam Goody. Your typical cramped, messy chain store, with good sales on chart records.

☞ **Virgin.** The first store to sell cut-price records. Owned by Richard Branson, who also owns an airline and movie concern. The Virgin Megastore on Oxford Street (14-30 Oxford Street, London W1N 7AB; tel. (071) 631-1234) is a huge complex offering CDs, tapes, records, books, videos, T-shirts—even a Virgin Travel Office and Keith Prowse ticket agent for plays and concerts. There's another megastore in Dublin, along the River Liffey next to USIT (14-18 Aston Quay).

☞ **Tower Records** (1 Piccadilly Circus, London W1R 8TR; tel. (071) 439-2500, tube: Piccadilly Circus). The largest store is in Piccadilly Circus; sells the *San Francisco Chronicle* (a week late), other newspapers, *Spy,* and *Rolling Stone,* in addition to tapes, records, CDs, and videos.

APPENDIX A

Study Abroad Resources

GENERAL

In the United States:

British Information Services (BIS)
845 Third Avenue
New York, NY 10022
United States
tel. (212) 752-8400

Publishes "Study in Britain," a short pamphlet on how to study abroad.

Bureau of Consular Affairs
Office of Passport Services
Department of State
Washington, DC 20520
United States
tel. (202) 647-0518

For U.S. passports.

Council on International Educational Exchange (CIEE)
205 East 42nd Street
New York, NY 10017
United States
tel. (212) 661-1414

Publishes several *occasional papers* on study abroad and international education, sells the International Student Identity Card, and runs Council Travel, a student travel agency offering cheap flights. Also publishes *Whole World Handbook for Work, Study and Travel Abroad* and issues work permits for Britain and Ireland. Contact CIEE for BUNAC information.

Department of State
Bureau of Public Affairs
2201 C Street NW
Washington, DC 20520
United States
tel. (202) 647-9606

Publishes *Background Notes* on different countries, which are four-page handouts detailing current events, regularly updated every few months.

Institute of International Education (IIE)
809 United Nations Plaza
New York, NY 10017
United States
tel. (212) 883-8200

Publishes *Study in the United Kingdom and Ireland* every two years, listing over 800 study abroad programs, and *Academic Year Abroad,* which lists programs worldwide. The latter is updated annually and is a more up-to-date source. IIE also advises students at its centers in Chicago, Denver, Houston, San Francisco, and New York.

Intercultural Press
Post Office Box 700
Yarmouth, ME 04096
United States
tel. (207) 846-5168

Publishes several guides dealing with study abroad, international education, and cross-cultural relations.

NAFSA: Association of International Educators
1860 19th Street NW
Washington, DC 20009
United States

Umbrella organization of individuals and organizations concerned with international education and study abroad. It holds an endless number of conferences (read David Lodge's *Small World* for the inside scoop). Write to *SECUSSA* (Section on U.S. Students Abroad) for more information.

In Canada:

Canadian Bureau for International Education (CBIE)
85 Albert Street, Suite 1400
Ottawa, Ontario K1P 6A4
Canada
tel. (613) 237-4820

Deals primarily with the concerns of foreign students in Canada, but does publish *What in the World Is Going On?* for Canadians interested in study overseas.

Passport Office
Department of External Affairs
125 Sussex Drive
Ottawa, Ontario K1A 0G2
Canada
tel. (613) 994-3500

For Canadian passports.

Travelcuts
171 College Street
Toronto, Ontario M5T 1P7
Canada
tel. (416) 979-2406

CIEE's main Council Travel office in Canada. Issues international student identity cards, handles some overseas work and study programs.

In Britain:

The British Council
10 Spring Gardens
London SW1A 2BN
United Kingdom
tel. (071) 930-8466

British government agency designed to promote understanding of Britain in other countries; runs scholarship programs and organizes educational exchanges; publishes *How to Live in Britain.*

British Universities Transatlantic Exchanges Committee (BUTEC)
c/o Central Bureau, Seymour Mews House
Seymour Mews
London W1H 9PE
United Kingdom
tel. (071) 486-5101

Organization concerned with promoting and monitoring transatlantic educational exchange. Publishes *Study in Britain,* a pamphlet in which each member university glowingly describes itself. Not every British university is a member of BUTEC.

Canadian High Commission
Canada House
Trafalgar Square   38 Grosvenor Street
London SW1Y 5BJ   London W1X 0A8
United Kingdom
tel. (071) 629-9492

The High Commission is open 9:00 A.M.-5:30 P.M., Monday to Friday, but there is a duty officer to answer the phone (in French and English) at all times.

Central Bureau for Educational Visits & Exchanges
Seymour Mews House
Seymour Mews
London W1H 0BE
United Kingdom
tel. (071) 486-5101

British government-financed organization that provides information on short-term educational visits, mainly for language study; publishes *Study Holidays,* a guide to short-term study options.

Colleges and Polytechnics Transatlantic Exchanges Committee
CAPTEC Secretariat
c/o Central Bureau, Seymour Mews House
Seymour Mews
London W1H 9PE
United Kingdom
tel. (071) 486-5101

An association of British public sector higher education institutions organized to promote colleges and polytechnics abroad.

Commonwealth Trust
18 Northumberland Avenue
London WC2N 5BJ
United Kingdom
tel. (071) 930-6733

Organizes special events for students from Commonwealth countries (e.g.,
Canada, Australia, New Zealand).

Consulate of Canada
Meclay Murray Spens
Solicitors
151 St. Vincent Street
Glasgow G2 5NJ
Scotland
tel. (041) 331 4416

Open 9:00 A.M.-5:00 P.M., Monday to Friday.

Council on International Educational Exchange (CIEE)
33 Seymour Place
London W1H 6AT
United Kingdom
tel. (071) 706-3008

See CIEE under "In the United States" listing. The London office cannot issue
BUNAC work permits—these must be purchased before leaving the States.

Council for National Academic Awards (CNAA)
344-354 Gray's Inn Road
London WC1X 8BP
United Kingdom
tel. (071) 278-4411

Traditionally awarded degrees to graduates of polytechnics. The Council
may not exist once the polys receive new university charters.

Fulbright Commission (U.S./U.K. Education Commission)
Educational Advisory Service
6 Porter Street
London W1M 2HR
United Kingdom
tel. (071) 486-1098

The Fulbright program was initiated by Arkansas Senator J. W. Fulbright, a Rhodes Scholar who arranged the sale of surplus U.S. military equipment after WWII in order to finance educational and cultural exchanges, postgraduate and postdoctoral scholarships, and midcareer fellowships. The London Commission offers a comprehensive library of U.S. university catalogs, graduate admissions test application forms (GRE, GMAT, MCAT), and professional advice on all matters relating to American education.

National Union of Students (NUS)
461 Holloway Road
London N7 6LJ
United Kingdom
tel. (071) 272-8900

Umbrella national student union that all university student unions belong to unless their members opt to drop out; campaigns for student rights; publicizes student (and nonstudent) issues; publishes *Overseas Student Handbook,* mainly a guide for their Overseas Student Officers.

Universities Central Council on Admissions (UCCA)
Post Office Box 28
Cheltenham, Glos GL50 3SA
United Kingdom
tel. (0242) 222444

Publishes *How to Apply for Admission to a University* and provides application forms for students, British and North American, planning to study for an undergraduate degree.

United Kingdom Council for Overseas Student Affairs (UKCOSA)
60 Westbourne Grove
London W2 5SH
United Kingdom
tel. (071) 229-9268

Advises overseas students and publishes a series of guidance notes on taxes (i.e., Poll Tax), immigration, visas, health insurance, work permits, etc. Operates an advisory service, Monday-Friday, 1:00 P.M.-4:00 P.M.

United States Consulate
3 Regent Terrace
Edinburgh
Scotland
tel. (031) 556-8315

Open 10:00 A.M.-12:00 P.M., 1:00 P.M.-4:00 P.M., Monday to Friday.

United States Embassy
24 Grosvenor Square
London W1A 1AE
United Kingdom
General Information Number: (071) 499-9000
American Citizenship and Passport Enquiries: (071) 491-3506

The embassy is open 8:30 A.M.-5:30 P.M., but it operates a 24-hour emergency phone service. You may need it for lost passports or extra passport pages (Passport Office open 8:30 A.M.-1:00 P.M., Monday to Friday). The embassy looks like a cross between a Holiday Inn and the front grille of a '57 Chevy. Impossible to miss, especially with Eisenhower glaring at you from the front steps.

In Ireland:

Canadian Embassy
65-68 St. Stephen's Green South
Dublin 2
Republic of Ireland
tel. (01) 781988

Open 10:00 A.M.-12:00 P.M., 2:00 P.M.-4:00 P.M., Monday to Friday.

Central Applications Office (CAO)
Tower House
Eglinton Street
Galway
Republic of Ireland
tel. (091) 63318, 63269

Provides application forms for Irish and North American students considering a full degree at an Irish (Republic) university.

Higher Education Authority
21 Fitzwilliam Square
Dublin 2
Republic of Ireland
tel. (01) 612748

Provides basic information on universities, colleges, and the Irish education system.

Irish Council for Overseas Students (ICOS)
41 Morehampton Road
Dublin 4
Republic of Ireland
tel. (01) 605233

Runs reception/orientation programs, advises on accommodation and welfare, and provides information on life in Ireland for overseas students. Offices are in Dublin but it has a staff member based in Galway. Council deals primarily with students from Third-World countries.

Union of Students in Ireland (USI)
16 North Great George Street
Dublin 1
Republic of Ireland
tel. (01) 786366

Umbrella national student union for Irish universities (including Northern Ireland), quite left-wing, so not all universities belong. In 1990, members included University College Dublin, Dublin City University, Trinity College Dublin, Queens University of Belfast, and the University of Ulster.

United States Consulate General
Queens House
Queen Street
Belfast
Northern Ireland
tel. (0232) 328239

Open 10:00 A.M.-12:00 P.M., 1:00 P.M.-4:00 P.M., Monday to Friday.

United States Embassy
42 Elgin Road
Ballsbridge
Dublin 4
Republic of Ireland
tel. (01) 688777

Open 8:30 A.M.-5:00 P.M., Monday to Friday.

RESOURCES FOR THE DISABLED

In the United States:

Mobility International U.S.
P.O. Box 3551
Eugene, OR 97403
United States
tel. (503) 343-1284

Mobility International publishes a series of leaflets for the disabled concerning work, study, and travel abroad. Ask for their *Guide to International Educational Exchange, Community Service, and Travel for Persons with Disabilities.*

In Britain and Ireland:

Mobility International
228 Borough High Street
London SE1 1JX
United Kingdom
tel. (071) 403-5688

Royal National Institute for the Blind
224 Great Portland Street
London W1 N6AA
United Kingdom
tel. (071) 388-1266

Royal Institute for the Deaf
105 Gower Street
London WCIE 6AH
United Kingdom
tel. (071) 387-8033

SKILL, National Bureau for Students with Disabilities
336 Brixton Road
London SW9 7AA
United Kingdom
tel. (071) 274-0565

SKILL is publishing the *Higher Education Access Guide*, a review of each university, polytechnic, and college of higher education with emphasis on accessibility and services available to students with disabilities, particularly wheelchair access. SKILL itself is a useful resource, and if it doesn't have the answers to your study-related questions, it can put you in touch with others who do.

Other organizations listed earlier in this appendix which provide information and advocacy for disabled students are the National Union of Students in both Britain and Ireland, the United Kingdom Council for Overseas Student Affairs, the Irish Council for Overseas Students, and the student union of the university to which you are applying. See chapter 1 for more information on facilities for the disabled.

APPENDIX B

Universities

UNIVERSITIES IN ENGLAND

Overseas Office
University of Aston
Aston Triangle
Birmingham B4 7ET
(021) 359-3611

JYA Studies Coordinator
Office of the Academic Secretary
University of Birmingham
Edgbaston
Birmingham B15 2TT
(021) 414-3344

Assistant International Students
Officer
International Students Office
University of Bath
Claverton Down
Bath BA2 7AY
(0225) 826800, 465200

Chairman
International Visiting Student's
Programme
University of Bradford
Bradford
West Yorkshire BD7 1DP
(0274) 733466

Director
Study Abroad Office
University of Bristol
12 Priory Road
Bristol BS8 1TU
(0272) 303030

Academic Secretary
University of Brunel
Uxbridge, Middlesex UB8 3PH
(0895) 74000
for Faculty of Social Sciences,
write to:
Inter-Study
42 Milsom Street
Bath BA1 1DN

Director
Visiting Students' Programme
University of Buckingham
Hunter Street
Buckingham MK18 1EG
(0280) 814080

University of Cambridge
Cambridge CB2 1TN
(0223) 337733

Assistant Registrar
City University
Northampton Square
London EC1V 0HB
(071) 253-4399

Director
Institute of European Studies
University of Durham
Durham DH1 3HP
(091) 374-2000

Visiting Students Officer
Visiting Students Office
University of East Anglia
The Registry
Norwich
Norfolk NR4 7TJ
(0603) 56161

Director of International
Programmes
University of Essex
Wivenhoe Park
Colchester CO4 3SQ
(0206) 873777

Admissions Officer
University of Exeter
Northcote House
The Queen's Drive
Exeter EX4 4QJ
(0392) 263263

External Relations Officer
University of Hull
Hull HU6 7RX
(0482) 46311

Head of International Office
The University of Keele
Keele
Staffordshire ST5 5BG
(0782) 621111

Head of Office for Undergraduate
Recruitment Services
The University of Kent at
Canterbury
Canterbury
Kent CT2 7NZ
(0227) 764000

Director
North American Programs
University of Lancaster
Lancaster LA1 4YW
(0524) 65201

Undergraduate Office (Admissions)
University of Leeds
Leeds LS2 9JT
(0532) 431751

International Liaison Officer
University of Leicester
University Road
Leicester LE1 7RH
(0533) 522522

Assistant Registrar
University of Liverpool
International Office
Senate House
Abercromby Square
Post Office Box 147
Liverpool L69 3BX
(051) 794-2071

University of London
Senate House
Malet Street
London WC1E 7HU
(071) 636-8000

Assistant Registrar
Loughborough University of Technology
Loughborough
Leicestershire LE11 3TU
(0509) 263171

Coordinator, MAP Office
University of Manchester
Arts Building
Manchester M13 9PL
(061) 275-2000

JYA Advisor
International Office
University of Newcastle-upon-Tyne
Old Library Building
Newcastle-upon-Tyne NE1 7RU
(091) 232-8511

International Office
University of Nottingham
University Park
Nottingham NG7 2RD
(0602) 484848

University of Oxford
Oxford OX1 2JD
(0865) 270000

Director
Visiting Students Office
University of Reading
Whiteknights
Reading RG6 2AH
(0734) 875123

The Director
Salford Semester
University of Salford
Manchester M5 4WT
(061) 736-5843

International Office
University of Sheffield
Western Bank
Sheffield S10 2TN
(0742) 768555

Assistant Registrar
University of Southampton
Highfield
Southampton SO9 5NH
(0703) 559122

Director
Occasional Students' Programmes
Office for Special Programmes
University of Surrey
Guildford
Surrey GU2 5XH
(0483) 571281

Director
North American Programmes
University of Sussex
Falmer, Brighton
East Sussex BN1 9RH
(0273) 606755

Co-ordinator
Visiting & Exchange Programmes
University of Warwick
International Office
Coventry CV4 7AL
(0203) 523523

Assistant Registrar
University of York
Heslington
York YO1 5DD
(0904) 430000

UNIVERSITIES IN WALES

Director
International Center
**University College of Wales,
Aberystwyth**
Old College
Aberystwyth
Dyfed SY23 2AX
(0970) 622081, 622083

Assistant Registrar
**University College of North
Wales, Bangor**
Bangor
Gwynedd LL57 2DG
(0248) 351151

International Office
University of Wales College Cardiff
52 Park Place
Cardiff CF1 3XA
(0222) 874000

Deputy Registrar
**St. David's University College,
Lampeter**
Lampeter
Dyfed SA48 7ED
(0570) 422351

Co-ordinator, U.S. Study Abroad
Office
University of Wales, Swansea
Singleton Park
Swansea SA2 8PP
(0792) 205678

UNIVERSITIES IN SCOTLAND

Associate Director
Overseas Office
University of Aberdeen
Regent Walk
Aberdeen AB9 1FX
(0224) 273503

Director, International Office
Heriot-Watt University
Lord Balerno Building
Riccarton
Edinburgh EH14 4AS
(031) 449-5111

Co-ordinator of Overseas Student
Affairs
University of Dundee
Dundee DD1 4HN
(0382) 23181

American Enrolment Officer/
Adviser
University of St. Andrews
College Gate
St. Andrews
Fife KY16 9AJ
(0334) 76161

Director
International Office
University of Edinburgh
6 Buccleuch Place
Edinburgh EH8 9LW
(031) 667-1011

JYA/Overseas Office
University of Stirling
Stirling FK9 4LA
(0786) 73171

Administrator
Office for Special Programmes
University of Glasgow
Glasgow G12 8QQ
(041) 339-8855

ISEP/JYA Coordinator, International Office
University of Strathclyde
McCance Building
Glasgow G1 1XQ
(041) 552-4400, x2912

UNIVERSITIES IN NORTHERN IRELAND

JYA Co-ordinator
**The Queen's University of
Belfast**
Admissions Office
Belfast BT7 1NN
(0232) 245133

Academic Registry
**University of Ulster at
Jordanstown**
Newtownabbey
County Antrim BT37 0QB
(0232) 365131

UNIVERSITIES IN THE REPUBLIC OF IRELAND

Admissions Officer
University College, Cork (UCC)
Cork
(021) 276871

Director, Junior Year Abroad
Programme
**University College, Dublin
(UCD)**
Belfield
Dublin 4
(01) 693244

Office of Academic Affairs
Dublin City University (DCU)
Glasnevin
Dublin 9
(01) 370077

Academic Secretary
**University College, Galway
(UCG)**
Galway
(091) 24411

Admissions Office
University of Limerick
Plassey Technological Park
Limerick
(061) 333644

Dean of International Affairs
Trinity College, Dublin
University of Dublin
Dublin 2
(01) 772941

IRISH REGIONAL TECHNICAL COLLEGES

RTC, Athlone, County Westmeath
(0904) 72647

RTC, Dublin Road, Galway
(091) 53161

RTC, Cork Road, Waterford
(051) 75934

RTC, Dundalk, County Loath
(042) 34785, 34879

RTC, Rossa Ave., Bishopstown, Cork
(021) 545222

RTC, Ballinode, Sligo
(071) 43261

RTC, Kilkenny Road, Carlow
(0503) 31324

RTC, Clash, Tralee, County Kerry
(066) 24666

University Map of
Britain and Ireland

Vocabulary

Thic lict ic intended to help you understand what's being said to you and what you read in the newspaper or hear on TV. But *be careful:* use some of these terms (especially those under "People," "Slang," and "Political Terms") with caution and common sense!

Welsh is spoken in many parts of Wales, especially in the north and northwest, and is actively promoted by the Welsh government. Since this often surprises North Americans arriving for a year abroad, a pronunciation guide and vocabulary list are provided at the end of this appendix.

Today's *Scots* is a mixture of English and *Scots Gaelic* ("Gallic"). Older forms of Scots were best popularized by Scotland's foremost poet, Robert Burns, who penned everything from "Auld Lang Syne" ("Long Ago," a popular folk song he transcribed, although many credit him as its author) to "Nine Inch Will Please a Lady." Pure Gaelic is still spoken, too, but only in remote areas of the western Highlands and islands. Glaswegians speak their own distinctive (read: unintelligible) form of Scots called *the patter.* Only the most common phrases have been included here.

An Guellacht are Irish-speaking areas, mostly in the west, where locals cling to their native language as strongly as the Welsh cling to theirs. *Irish Gaeilge* ("Gaylik") pronunciation is exceedingly difficult (there are several more vowels than in English) and varies with the province, so get a native speaker to help you out and buy a phrase book. Try saying a few words in Irish Gaeilge and you'll break the ice and make even the most reserved person smile.

VOCABULARY

Food and Drink

afters dessert (a cooked, sweet dish; refers only to fruit or pudding)
aubergine eggplant
bangers and mash sausage and mashed potatoes
bannock a round, flat oatmeal cake (Scottish)
bap bun, an oversize granary bun
barmbrack fruit loaf (Irish)
Barr's Irn Bru a sweet, sugary, Glaswegian soft drink
Bath Oliver a kind of unsweetened biscuit or soda cracker, named after William Oliver, a doctor from the city of Bath
beetroot beet
bevvy alcohol, to drink (Glaswegian)
bitter smooth, dark beer served at close to room temperature
black pudding a moist patty made of pork, fat, and pig's blood, served with breakfast (*black sausage* in Ireland)
black velvet Guinness and champagne
boiled sugar rock candy (Irish)
Bovril beef bouillon (trade name)
boxty potato pancake (Irish)
brown sauce a mix of a Worcestershire-like sauce, vinegar, and other ingredients, popular on chips and haggis
bubble and squeak fried mashed potato and cabbage
buttery cafeteria, canteen
butty bread and butter sandwich (a *chip butty* is a french fry sandwich)
chips french fries, only thicker and greasier
cider fermented apple cider
coddle potato, sausage and bacon stew (Irish)
colcannon kale (tough cabbage), boiled potato, and onion mixed and mashed together; often served at Halloween in Ireland
Cornish pastie meat and vegetables in a pastry pouch; originates from the English county of Cornwall
courgette zucchini
cream slice pastry with cream
crisps potato chips
crubeen pig's feet, a Cork specialty

cruesli a granola-type cereal, with sugar

diamond white cider and white wine

digestive biscuits plain cookies

the Dog Newcastle Brown Ale (or "Newkie Brown"), a popular student brew; this term is used mostly in the Newcastle-upon-Tyne area

drooth thirst (Glaswegian)

drusheen tripe (cow intestines), often boiled in milk (Irish)

Dundee cake fruit cake (Scottish)

Edinburgh rock rock candy

electric soup methylated spirits and cheap red wine (Glaswegian, naturally)

faggot meatball

farl baked triangle-shaped bread with one curved side, made from a baking soda and buttermilk base; varieties include wheaten farls, treacle farls, soda farls; from the Irish "fardel," meaning fourth part or one-fourth of a round cake

gammon ham

ginger a carbonated soft drink (Glaswegian)

glass in Ireland, a half-pint of beer or a large (double) measure of spirits

guest ale a special ale served in a pub for a short time only

haggis sheep guts in sheep stomach, the national dish of Scotland

hauf and a hauf a shot of whiskey and a glass of beer (Glaswegian)

heavy strong bitter served in Scotland

Horlicks hot malted milk (trade name)

hot whiskey whiskey with cloves, brown sugar, and slice of lemon (Irish)

Irish coffee coffee with brown sugar, whipped cream, and whiskey

jar pint

jelly Jell-O

kebab Turkish meal made from minced ham and beef rolled on a skewer, cooked slowly, then sliced and served in a pita pocket with salad

lager light pilsner beer

lemonade carbonated water with lemon juice (e.g., 7-Up, Sprite)

Marmite (trade name) bitter yeast extract; spread on toast

mild light bitter popular among Mancunians

mince ground beef, hamburger meat

minerals soft drinks or sodas in Ireland

neep turnip

Newkie Brown Newcastle Brown Ale, also called "the Dog"

off-license, offy liquor store licensed to sell alcoholic beverages for consumption off the premises

perry an alcoholic pear drink, served primarily in Devon and Cornwall

pickle strong, brownish, pickle relish, commonly served with pub meals

pie, mash, and liquor spiced mince pie, mashed potato, and a thin green gravy made from vinegar, spices, parsley and peas; Cockney specialty

ploughman's lunch cheese, bread, salad, pickle (served in pubs); the result
   of an ad campaign in the 1960s, thoroughly unbeknownst to ploughmen
potato cakes fried Irish cakes made from mashed potato and flour
poteen (pronounced "pocheen") Irish moonshine whiskey
pulses peas, beans, lentils
purple nasty lager, cider, black currant, and a shot of Pimm's
rasher slice of bacon
rattler snakebite with Southern Comfort instead of black currant
real ale ale brewed according to traditional methods; cask-conditioned ale
Ribena (trade name) black currant drink (other flavors now available)
samosa deep-fried Indian pastry stuffed with spicy meat or vegetables
savoury highly flavored foods, composed chiefly of grease and meat, served
   as an hors d'oeuvre or dessert; includes everything from sausage rolls
   to beef crisps; often offered at tea
scone a flat, quick bread cut into triangles and baked on a sheet or cooked
   on a griddle
Scotch egg hard-boiled egg, surrounded by breaded sausage meat
scouse a Liverpudlian stew made with vegetables, meat, and spices (the
   reason why Liverpudlians are called "scousers")
scrumpy strong flat cider brewed in the West Country
shandy traditionally bitter and 7-Up, but in London often lager and 7-Up
shepherd's pie minced beef and carrots with mashed potato on top
shortbread a sweet Scottish cookie made with flour, butter, and sugar
   (hint: don't buy it in gift shops or train stations or airports. It's widely
   available and cheaper everywhere else)
snakebite cider and lager, often served with "black" (black currant)
spotted dick dessert with currants
squash highly concentrated juice (make sure you add water!)
starter appetizer
stottie a thick sandwich made with one-quarter of a stottycake, a flat
   brown loaf made in Newcastle-upon-Tyne
stout dark, thick, bitter, creamy brew (e.g., Guinness, Murphy's)
tattie potato
tattie bread very heavy potato bread (Northern Ireland)
toad in the hole sausage in a Yorkshire pudding (popover)
treacle molasses
VW vodka and white wine
Yorkshire pudding popover

Clothing

anorak parka, ski jacket
barbour jacket oiled, rainproof overcoat
baseball boots basketball sneakers (usually Converse)

bespoke hand-tailored (i.e., a suit, jacket)
braces suspenders
brogues heavy shoes
brolley umbrella
Durex condom; also known as *jiffies* and *johnnies*
green wellies rubber boots, similar in function and reputation to the L.L.
  Bean boat shoe
jumper sweater
knickers women's underpants
nappy diaper
pants underwear
plus fours knickerbockers (knee-length pants)
sporran hanging pouch worn with a Scottish kilt
suspenders garters
tattersall shirt checked, tweed jacket
tights panty hose, nylons
trainers sneakers
trews long Scottish tartan pants
twin set matching woolen vest and sweater; worn by middle-aged women
  or aspiring female corporate executives
underskirt slip
vest undershirt

Housing

aga coal-burning stove
bedsitter/bedsit one-room apartment in someone's home
bog rest room
bog roll toilet paper
cooker kitchen stove
council housing low-income housing administered by local government
detached house house (free-standing)
duvet comforter with a washable, removable sheet cover
first floor first floor up from ground floor (second floor)
flannel face cloth
flat apartment
ground floor first floor
larder pantry, cupboard
lift elevator
loo rest room
mews the cobblestoned courtyards of old stables and servants' living
  quarters, now converted to expensive houses and flats (especially popular
  because the old stables can be used as garages)
paternoster continuously moving elevator

power point wall socket
self-catering accommodation with a kitchen; no meal plan
semi-detached house two-family house (shares a common wall)
shaver point special wall socket for electric shavers only
terraced house row house, attached condominium
traditional hall university accommodation with a meal plan
w.c. rest room (from water closet)

Transportation, Travel and Places

A to Z (pronounced "a to zed") map; book of city maps
Alba Gaelic term for Scotland
alight get off
the Barras Glasgow's famous outdoor market
bearpit a pub where loud, drunk, young men ("bears") hang out
the Bogside Catholic area of (London)Derry
boot trunk (of car)
bonnet hood (of car)
Bord Fáilte the Irish Tourist Board
Bus Éireann the national bus company of Ireland
caravan trailer
car park parking lot
carriage individual car of a train
chapel Catholic church
church Protestant church
circus the term for certain large traffic circles (e.g., Piccadilly Circus)
the City the financial center of London
close dead end, cul-de-sac
Connaught western Irish province encompassing Galway and several Gaeilge
    (Irish)-speaking areas (e.g., Connemara)
dander short walk, stroll (Northern Ireland)
derv diesel
Donegal Road Protestant area of Belfast
dual carriageway divided highway
Erin Gaelic term for Ireland
estate car station wagon
Falls Road Catholic area of Belfast
firth an estuary, a big inlet that becomes a river
flyover overpass
Gorbals formerly a notorious, gangster-spawning area of Glasgow; means
    "beautiful town" in Gaelic
high street main street; shopping area
Highlands the mountainous northwestern upland region of Scotland
howe a hollow; a low basin

Iarnród Éireann Irish Rail
indicator turn signal (in a car)
kirk church (Scottish)
lay-by paved shoulder
Leinster eastern Irish province that includes Dublin
loch lake
lorry truck
lough lake
Lowlands less mountainous regions in the south and east of Scotland, including Glasgow and Edinburgh
mere lake (England)
minicab unlicensed taxi run by a private company, often ordered by phone
minster cathedral
moor wet, boggy, infertile area dominated by grasses and heather
motorway highway, freeway
munroes small mountains, peaks over 3,000 feet
Munster southern Irish province encompassing Limerick and Cork
no go area dangerous, high-crime area; slum
Old Course the seaside site in St. Andrews where the Royal and Ancient Golf Club invented the game of golf in 1754
pavement sidewalk
pelican crossing crosswalk
petrol gas
Republic the Republic of Ireland
Robin Reliant three-wheeled car
roundabout traffic circle
saloon the deck (upper or lower) of a double-decker bus
shire county
silencer muffler
single carriageway undivided highway
single ticket one-way ticket
the Six Counties six of the nine counties of Ulster, that make up Northern Ireland (see "Ulster")
southern Ireland the Republic of Ireland; this term is used by many English to refer to the Republic
sterling area Northern Ireland (where only British sterling is accepted); Irish Republic newspapers print separate prices for Ireland and the "sterling area"
subway pedestrian underpass
tailback bumper-to-bumper traffic
tube subway, metro, underground
Ulster northern Irish province consisting of nine counties, six of which now form the U.K.-administered region of Northern Ireland: Antrim, Armagh, Down, Fermanagh, (London)Derry, and Tyrone
windscreen windshield

wynd (pronounced as in "wind your watch") a narrow lane (Scottish)
zebra crossing crosswalk

Political Terms

An Taoiseach (pronounced "An Teeshik") the Irish Prime Minister
Butcher's Apron Northern Irish Catholic term for the Union Jack (U.K. flag)
CND Campaign for Nuclear Disarmament
community charge euphemistic term for the soon to be defunct Poll Tax
Dáil Éireann (pronounced "Doil Erin") the elected, lower house of the Irish Parliament (*Oireachtas*)
Downing Street where the British Prime Minister lives (Number 10)
Easter Uprising unsuccessful attempt to throw out the British on Easter of 1916
Fenian member of a nineteenth-century independence movement, now used by Northern Irish Protestants to mean Catholic (Northern Ireland)
Free State predecessor of the Irish Republic, existed 1922 to 1948, used in Northern Ireland to designate the Republic as a sign of deliberate, contemptuous ignorance
House of Commons the elected, lower house of the British Parliament
House of Lords the unelected, upper house of the British Parliament
Leinster House where the *Dáil* and *Seanad* (Irish Parliament) meet, on Kildare Street in Dublin
loyalist someone in favor of Northern Ireland remaining part of the U.K., often Protestant
MI5 the British Secret Service; similar in function to the CIA, allegedly based in the Orwellian Thames-side Shell Building
MI6 the British internal secret security police, concerned with domestic criminal activity
MoD Ministry of Defense
nationalist someone in favor of a united Ireland (Northern Ireland)
New Consensus people in the Republic of Ireland advocating an end to violence by the IRA
NIPF Northern Ireland Police Federation
Noraid main Irish-American republican support group, known to funnel money to the provisional IRA
OBE Order of the British Empire, political honor annually awarded by the prime minister
Oireachtas, Houses of the Oireachtas the Irish Parliament, based in Leinster House in Dublin, consisting of an elected lower house (the *Dáil*) and an unelected upper house (the *Seanad*)
Parliament, Houses of Parliament located in Westminster in London; consists of an elected lower house (the House of Commons) and an

unelected upper house (House of Lords); when most people say "Parliament," they're referring to the House of Commons

Poll Tax a controversial government tax on every person over eighteen;
the amount of tax depends on the number of community services your
district provides; the original Poll Tax was repealed in 1381

rates property tax (now replaced by the Poll Tax)

republican someone in favor of a united Ireland, often Catholic

RUC Royal Ulster Constabulary; Northern Ireland police force

Seanad (pronounced "Shenad") the Irish Senate, the unelected upper house
of Parliament (*Oireachtas*)

security forces British troops (UDR) and the Northern Irish police (RUC)

Special Powers Act British law that gives the Ulster Defense Regiment (UDR)
wide powers of detention in Northern Ireland and throughout the U.K.

TD Teachta Dala (pronounced "Techta Dala"), member of the lower house
of the Irish Parliament (the *Dáil*)

the Crown the government, which even today is headed by the monarchy

UDR Ulster Defense Regiment; formed in early 1970s; British army regiment based in Northern Ireland; each county has its own unit (e.g., Co.
Tyrone is 6UDR (6th battalion, Ulster Defense Regiment)); some UDR
members thought to be sympathetic to the aims of the UVF

unionist someone in favor of Northern Ireland remaining part of the U.K.,
often Protestant

Westminster London borough where Parliament is based

White Paper a policy statement issued by the government

Political Parties and Organizations

British:

Conservative Party one of the two main political parties in Britain, considered right-wing; also called the Tory Party; famous recent prime
ministers include Edward Heath and Margaret Thatcher

the Green Party small environmentalist political party

Labour Party one of the two main political parties in Britain, considered
to lean to the left, with a far-left (or "loony left") contingent

LDP (Liberal Democratic Party) a small, center-left political party

Militant small, far-left political party, accused by the Tories of causing
every one of Britain's woes

Monster Raving Loonies the largest of several independent political parties; do quite well in many elections (polled more support than the SDP
in 1990, which helped hasten the SDP's demise)

PD Progressive Democrats, a small political party

SDP the now defunct Social Democratic Party, once a splinter group of
the Labour Party led by Dr. David Owen

SNP the Scottish National party, which calls for independence and devolution from the United Kingdom
SWP Socialist Workers party, small, far-left political organization
WP Workers party, a small political party

Irish:

CRF Catholic Reaction Force; small Irish terrorist group
Cummann na mBan women's wing of the IRA
DUP Democratic Unionist party, an official Irish political party led by the Protestant Reverend Ian Paisely
Fianna Fáil (FF) (pronounced "Feena Foil") one of the two main political parties in the Republic of Ireland; dramatically translates to "Soldiers of Destiny"
Fine Gael (FG) (pronounced "Finna Gale") one of the two main political parties in the Irish Republic; translates to "Race of the Irish"
INLA Irish National Liberation Army; small republican terrorist group
IPLO Irish People's Liberation Organization; small republican terrorist group
IRA Irish Republican Army; the main republican terrorist group; "*Oglaigh na Éireann*" in Irish Gaeilge
Na Fianna Éireann IRA Youth Brigade
PIRA Provisional Irish Republican Army; terrorist arm of the IRA; see "provisionals"
provisionals, provos, PIRA hard-core arm of the IRA; carry out most terrorist activities; advocate violence
Red Hand Commandos small, violent, Irish loyalist splinter group
Sinn Féin official political arm of the Irish Republican Army (IRA); translates to "Ourselves Alone"
UDF Ulster Defense Force; small loyalist terrorist group
UFF Ulster Freedom Fighters; small loyalist terrorist group
UUP Ulster Unionist party, an official political party
UVF Ulster Volunteer Force; loyalist terrorist group; advocates and practices violence against the IRA

Services, Sports, Media and Entertainment

abseiling rappeling; climbing down buildings with ropes
advert advertisement
An Óige (pronounced "An Oyga") the Irish Youth Hostel Association
An Post Irish postal service
BBC British Broadcasting Company
the Beeb the BBC
Black Maria police van

Boxing Day traditional holiday on the day after Christmas; servants used to receive boxes of leftover food

building societies savings and loans, but with cashpoint machines, checking services, and (often) higher interest rates than banks

busker street performer

call box phone booth

camogie rough, hockey-like game for girls played with a *hurley* (stick) and *sliodor* (puck); boy's version called *hurling*

carrier bag shopping bag

cashpoint bank machine; cash machine; ATM

casualty department emergency room

céilidh (pronounced "kaylee") traditional Scots dancing (like square dancing, "but not square.")

chemist pharmacy

chit receipt

constabulary county police force; regional police force

country dancing Scottish dancing, more complicated than céilidhs

creche day-care nursery

current account checking account

deposit account savings account

dosh cash

draughts checkers (the game)

FA Cup Football Association Cup Final; the Superbowl for English soccer fans (there's also a Scottish FA Cup Final—both are held in May)

Fir Irish Gaeilge for men's toilet

five-a-side informal soccer played with five people on each team

fleadh Irish Gaeilge for "feast"; often refers to a large arts or music festival

football soccer (NOTE: people rarely use the term "soccer," a dead giveaway for North Americans)

GIRO check welfare check; a payment drawn on a postal checking account

highland dancing solo Scottish dancing

hill-climbing big, heathery, craggy mountain climbing ("not just hills")

hire to rent

hooley wild and crazy party (Glaswegian)

hurling rough, hockey-like game for boys played with a *hurley* (stick) and *sliodor* (puck); girl's version called *camogie*

ironmonger hardware store

left luggage place to store your luggage at an airport, in a train station, etc.

Mná Irish Gaeilge for women's toilet

Mod, Gaelic Mod highland and island choral group competition held in October in a different part of the country each year

morris dancing popular and exhausting English dance performed by men wearing costumes and bells; often an English university club activity

naughts and crosses tic-tac-toe

newsagent stationery store; sells cards, candy, newspapers, and magazines

NHS National Health Service, Britain's socialized medical service

Old Firm the "institution" of Glaswegian football - the Rangers and Celtics

pantomime a fun, campy version of a well-known fairy tale performed around Christmas and New Year's in Scotland

piped TV cable TV; written as "pTV" in television scheduling guides

pitch sports ground, usually a soccer or cricket field

popmobility aerobics (Scottish)

post code zip code

queue line (pronounced 'q')

quid pound, £ (money)

RTE Radio Telefis Éireann, the main, government-owned radio and television network in Ireland

service till ATM; teller window in a bank

shinty wildly dangerous Irish/Scots form of hockey, where the ball can travel above your waist; similar to the Irish game of "hurling"

surgery doctor's or dentist's office

ta thanks

tattoo military parade on the grounds of Edinburgh Castle

television license document needed in order to operate a TV set, currently over £70 for a color set in Britain

Test Match international cricket competition that can last up to five days

the Old Bill the police; Robert Peel developed the police force, but the prime minister at the time responsible for enforcement was William Pitt ("Old Bill")

till cash register

trolley shopping cart

uillean Irish bagpipes; means "elbow" in Irish Gaeilge

VAT Value Added Tax, sales tax

Education

A-levels advanced examinations in specific subjects taken in England, Wales, and Northern Ireland at eighteen or nineteen; usually three required for university entrance

AS-levels advanced supplemental exams, more broadly based than A-levels, acceptable requirements for British students seeking admission to English, Welsh, and Northern Irish universities; can submit either AS-levels or A-levels

Aula Maxima main college auditorium in Ireland; Latin for "large hall"

AUT Association of University Teachers

calendar bible of university rules and regulations

central institution polytechnic in Scotland (see *polys* below)

CNAA Council for National Academic Awards, awards academic degrees to graduates of polytechnics

college institution of higher education within a university; also a special art or technical school, where students go to prepare for their A-level exams; also called a "further education college" or "sixth form college"

comprehensive school public school

CSE Certificate of Secondary Education examinations, lower than O-levels, no longer exists (replaced by GCSE)

ents entertainments, gigs, performances; name of entertainment committee in a student union (you'll find an "Ents Officer")

essay a long piece of researched work, 2,000-5,000 words (definitely not what North Americans mean by essay)

faculty academic department

first degree undergraduate degree

further education college see *college* and *sixth form*

GCSE General Certificate of Secondary Education examination, combining and replacing O-levels and CSEs

gown university robe, similar in style to a U.S. graduation robe, worn by men and women at formal dinners, balls, and other special events

grant system government tuition grant and a living grant for college students; being gradually phased out

guild student union

highers examinations taken in Scotland at about seventeen years of age, necessary for university entrance; similar to U.S. AP exams

honours course specialized degree course in Scotland, usually four years or longer

intermediate certificate granted in Ireland after taking intermediate exams at sixteen (similar to British "O-levels"); must be taken before leaving school

intermediate exams exams taken at age sixteen in Ireland

joint honors double major

junior common room (JCR) a group that organizes social activities in a hall; also the main bar in a college or dorm

JYA Junior Year Abroad

leaving certificate high school diploma, necessary for Irish university admission, granted after taking leaving exams at age seventeen or eighteen

leaving exams final exams taken after completing Irish secondary school

lecturers comparable to assistant professors in North America

matric card student ID card (Scottish)

mixed hall coed dorm

National University of Ireland includes University College Dublin (UCD), University College Cork (UCC), University College Galway (UCG), and St. Patrick's College at Maynooth

new universities those built in the 1960s to open higher education to more students; often concrete and glass structures on hills on the outskirts of towns

NIHEs National Institutes of Higher Education in Ireland, no longer in existence; University of Limerick and Dublin City University used to be NIHEs but are now full-fledged universities

NUS National Union of Students; umbrella federation of British and Northern Irish university student unions. Every union is automatically a member unless a majority of students vote to opt out

O-levels ordinary examinations taken at sixteen in a variety of subjects (now replaced by the GCSE)

ordinary course general degree course in Scotland, usually three years' duration

Oxbridge Oxford and Cambridge

personal tutor faculty member given the task of looking after a student's academic progress; sometimes called a "moral tutor"

pigeonhole campus mailbox

polys, polytechnics higher educational institutions that focus on practical subjects and the arts; polytechnic academic awards are made by the Council for National Academic Awards (CNAA); polys are now in the process of becoming fully chartered universities

practical lab

professor usually, but not always, the head of an academic department; a privileged title

prospectus college catalog

public school private, prep school

Rag student charity organization that runs an annual fund-raising week (Rag Week)

read to major in (e.g., "I'm reading History")

readers university academics promoted on the basis of their published work; educational status similar to that of professors in the United States; sometimes they teach classes, but are considered so important they're supposed to spend most of their time deep in thought

rector the nominal head of a Scottish university elected by the students every three or four years, who functions as their personal spokesperson and liaison with the administration

redbricks large, civic universities established in the late nineteenth/early twentieth century, often constructed of red brick

revise to study (for an exam)

rubber eraser

SA Students' Association, Scots term for Student Union; political arm is the *SRC*, or Students' Representative Council

sandwich course an extra fourth year of study spent working in industry or taking classes at a university abroad

senior lecturers comparable to associate professors in the U.S.

sixth form a college where students prepare for A-levels before going on to university; a separate "tier" of education falling between secondary and higher education

soc society, student club

third-level education Irish higher or university-level education

tutorial small study group; a lecturer (or grad student, reader, or professor) and one to ten students

UCCA Universities Central Council on Admissions, a clearinghouse institution that accepts applications to universities; anyone applying for an undergraduate degree applies through UCCA

UGM Union General Meeting, where students voice their concerns to the union executive

uni university

union campus political organization to which every student belongs; also the union building with student bars, shops; sometimes called "guild"

USI Union of Students in Ireland (*Aontas na Macléinn* in *Éireann*)

Slang and Dirty Words

The following list is for your information only. It is unwise to use these words in conversation until you are *absolutely certain* how, when, and with whom to do so.

boke to vomit
bollocks bullshit, balls
bugger off get the hell away; f— off
cock-up screw-up
fanny cunt (Scottish)
gear marijuana, hash; dope
git/get jerk
goer a woman who puts out; "a woman who just goes"
horny sexy, good-looking (e.g., "That bloke's horny" = "He's good-looking")
Joe Soap marijuana, hash; dope (from Cockney rhyming slang)
knob dick (Scottish)
laingered drunk
mankered drunk, tired
mashed stoned
paralytic drunk
peckish hungry
pillock jerk
pissed drunk
plonker jerk
poof(tah) faggot
prat jerk

rat-arsed drunk
roger screw
shag screw
shite shit, crap
skulled drunk
slag slut
slapper slut
smashed broke; drunk
snog kiss and cuddle
sod off piss off
stotious extremely drunk
throw up your ring to vomit, to puke
ticked off told off, scolded
tit asshole
tosser asshole (also masturbator)
wally idiot, jerk
wanker most offensive way to say asshole; masturbator
willy penis

People

Aberdonian from Aberdeen
Aussie Australian
bairn child (Scottish)
ban-garda policewoman (Irish)
barrister trial lawyer
bear noisy, heavy drinking young man (Glaswegian)
Billy Boys Northern Irish Protestants (after Protestant William of Orange)
bird young woman
bloke guy ("guy" is more common in Scotland)
bobby policeman
Bovver boy type of style characterized by baggy jeans, big black shoes, T-shirt, and short haircut that sweeps up in the front
Brummie person from Birmingham
casuals teenage thugs in Scotland with flared jeans and slicked-back hair who listen to house music and beat people up
child minder babysitter
constable policeman (Scottish)
dafs, daffodils Welsh
dipper pickpocket (Irish)
Dundonian from Dundee
eejit idiot (Irish)
Frog French person (derogatory)
fur coat and no knickers person who acts like he or she has money but doesn't

garda policeman (Irish)
gardai (pronounced "gardee") police (Irish)
Geordie person from Newcastle-upon-Tyne; also a strong Newcastle dialect, with roots in Norwegian
girl guide girl scout
Glaswegian from Glasgow
gombeen man
gothics/goths people in black who paint their faces white
GP general practitioner, doctor
hallion hooligan
hen woman (Scottish)
hinny woman (Geordie)
hooligans same as in North America, but especially used to describe English football (soccer) supporters
Hooray Henrys yuppies
HRH His or Her Royal Highness
jaffa Protestant in Northern Irish Catholic slang (Northern Ireland)
Jimmy what everyone in Glasgow will call you, even if your name is Mel
joiner carpenter
Kevins and Tracys and Sharons tasteless, flashy; class term denoting working-class people who earn money and buy cheap, tacky clothes
Kiwi New Zealander
knacker down 'n' out or homeless person (Irish)
lager lout a *yob*; an uneducated, heavy drinking, loutish fellow who gets into and starts plenty of drunken brawls
Leeks, Leekies Welsh
loon boy (Aberdeen)
macam, macam and tacam person from Sunderland; from "make 'em and take 'em," or manufacturing (Geordie term)
Mancunian, Mankie person from Manchester
Manx from the Isle of Man
mardy arses softies, weaklings (Mancunian term)
mature student resumed education student
MEP Member of European Parliament
Mick Catholic or Irish (derogatory)
millie girl who wears lots of makeup, short skirts; a tease; tart
MP Member of Parliament
nyaff jerk (Scottish)
O yahs yuppies, *Sloane Rangers, Hooray Henrys*
OAP old age pensioner, senior citizen
occasional student overseas student spending a term or year abroad; JYA
orangies Protestants (Northern Ireland)
Paddy Irish person (derogatory)
page 3 girl topless model in Rupert Murdoch's daily tabloid, *The Sun*
papist Catholic (derogatory) (Northern Ireland)

pavement dweller homeless person
pc police constable; policeman
piss artist heavy drinker; a person who, when drunk, starts talking crap
PM Prime Minister
prod Protestant (derogatory) (Northern Ireland)
punter an average Joe, an ordinary person ("one of the punters")
quine girl (Aberdeen)
rahs yuppies
redundant, to be made redundant unemployed; to become unemployed
sassenachs the English, or Saxons (Scottish)
Scouser Liverpudlian
seanachai Irish Gaeilge for storyteller
Sloane Ranger yuppie, preppie, upmarket *lager lout* (name comes from
   Sloane Square, an expensive shopping area of London)
solicitor lawyer
spiv opportunist; untrustworthy entrepreneur
spod nerd
squaddies soldiers
stoater, a richt stoater a stunning woman; hot babe (Glaswegian)
swot to study; someone who always studies
taffy person from south Wales (the River Taff runs through Cardiff)
tinkers traveling persons, itinerants, travelers; have their own association
toff member of the upper class
Tory member or supporter of the Conservative party
tout scalper (sells theater and concert tickets for a profit)
union hack (usually) left-wing student into union politics
VC vice chancellor, the corporate head of a university
victualler butcher
ween baby
whore (pronounced "whoor") a friendly, affectionate term used among
   men
womble antilitter crusader
yah southern English Oxbridge reject attending an ancient Scots university like St. Andrews, Edinburgh, Glasgow or Aberdeen
yob uneducated, violent, and sometimes racist hooligan

Expressions

are you getting? are you being served? (in a pub or restaurant)
Auld Lang Syne long ago (Scottish)
awa' wi' it drunk, thick (Glaswegian)
awa' wi' the fairies out of touch; out of it (Glaswegian)
bang out of order too drunk and getting out of hand
behave ("bee-ave") control yourself, chill out (Liverpudlian)

bugger it to hell with it
bugger (naff, sod) all nothing, zero, zip (as in "I haven't done bugger all today")
bunk off, done a bunk run off before having to answer or do something; to play truant
céad míle fáilte one hundred thousand welcomes (Irish Gaeilge saying)
chat up to pick up (a person)
dauner to stroll (Glaswegian)
doss about laze around
English disease football hooliganism; expression used by Europeans to describe the offensive, violent behavior of many English soccer fans
Erin Go Bragh! Long Live Ireland!
feck what polite ladies say instead of f—k (Irish)
flash a fag offer a cigarette
for flipsake polite way to say for Christ's sake (Irish)
ge's a break give me a break
Glasgow kiss a headbutt to the nose (watch out if you're wearing the wrong colors on the day of a big football match)
go for a slash take a piss
grass (on someone) to fink on someone
half (time) half past (time) (e.g., "half nine" = 9:30)
Happy Hogmanay! Happy New Year! (Scottish)
hump to carry
I dinnae ken I don't know (Scottish)
in a strop in a bad mood
in cloud cuckoo land out in left field, crazy, out of touch
it's a soft day it's raining tolerably (Irish)
keep your pecker up keep cheerful
knock up stop by, visit, or wake up with a knock on one's door (England)
lash, it's lashing out rain, it's raining heavily (Irish)
light name bad reputation (e.g., "you'll get a light name if you go there") (Irish)
like a fart in a trance in a daze, out of it (Glaswegian)
nick to steal; also a slang expression for pound (£)
och aye the noo a takeoff on the strange way the English think the Scots speak; supposed to mean "yes, indeed"
on the bevvy out drinking Scottish)
on the stew on the drink
on yer bike get out of here; piss off
orientate to orient yourself
OTT over the top; too much
out your face drunk (Scottish)
patter Glaswegian speech
piss about mess about

richt right (Scottish)

ring job a couple destined to get married (Irish)

row, give you a row lecture, give you a lecture; to argue

send someone up set someone up as the butt of a joke

skive off blow off work

slag someone off put someone down

slan goodbye (from the Irish Gaeilge)

slobber (someone/something) to bad-mouth someone/something

sound good (e.g., "sound, mate, sound" = "that's good")

spend a penny take a piss

suss something/someone **out** to find out the truth about something/someone

take the mickey make fun of someone, tease someone

take the piss make fun of someone, usually in a friendly way

take these wee notions to get these ideas (e.g., "I take these wee notions to go to America") (Irish)

the Troubles euphemistic term for the situation in Northern Ireland

vet to question; to interrogate

tuck in start eating

what's the crack? what's up?

whinge to whine

why aye yes (Geordie term)

wind someone up to aggravate someone, usually in a friendly way, by lying to them

Description

bee-heided light-headed, hung over (Glaswegian)

bevvied drunk (Glaswegian)

bonny pretty, handsome

brill from "brilliant"—great

canny good, as in "a canny lad" (a good guy) (Geordie term)

cheeky always playing pranks; saying or doing funny, bold, pointed things

dead ace totally awesome

dead hard extremely tough (also *rock hard*)

dead sound totally awesome

dead very (e.g., "dead sound" = "excellent")

dear expensive

dodgy unreliable (things); unscrupulous (people)

dosy easy, lazy

dote cute

double-barreled (name) hyphenated name (for example, Mr. Faichney-Reid)

downmarket poor, cheap
gobsmacked stunned, shocked
grotty run-down, gross
guttered drunk
Kelvinside posh, classy, pretentious (refers to an expensive area of Glasgow)
kip sleazy place, a hole; also, to sleep or nap
knacked Scots form of "knackered"; exhausted
knackered worn-out, broken (things); tired (people)
manky soiled, unwholesome
naff useless
preggers pregnant
rock hard extremely tough (also *dead hard*)
scotch this refers to whisky or eggs but *not* people!
Sharony kitch, tacky (see *Kevins and Tracys and Sharons* under "People")
skint broke
steaming drunk
stroppy argumentative, bitchy
tick on credit
upmarket classy, expensive, ritzy
wonky unstable

Miscellany

Armalite the American-made, self-repeating, semiautomatic weapon of choice for the provisional IRA
bank holiday national holiday
billion a million millions (1,000,000,000,000), or one trillion; but the North American meaning (a thousand millions, or 1,000,000,000) has caught on in British newspapers and television
biro ball point pen
blower telephone (Irish)
bruscar Irish Gaeilge term for litter (written on all the trash cans)
cellotape Scotch tape
claddagh old Irish wedding ring with two hands holding a heart with a crown; a popular tourist item
crackers glittery wrapped tubes containing prizes and gifts; you pull on each end, the tube explodes and the gifts fall out; available at special occasions like Christmas
Doc Martens black army boots that every student owns
drawing pin tack
dummy pacifier (for a baby)
fag cigarette; also a younger public (i.e., private boarding) school student made to perform chores for older students

fortnight two weeks (from "fourteen nights")

free house a pub not owned by a single brewery; usually offers a wider selection of beers

fullstop period (at the end of a sentence)

gob mouth

golliwog representation of a black man, an allegedly racist symbol of the Robertson's jam company; now called "golly" ("wog" was the racist portion, although many remain legitimately upset that all the company did in response to protest was change the name on their jam jars)

inver mouth of (e.g., Inverness = "the mouth of the River Ness")

kip sleep, nap

licensed, fully licensed able to sell intoxicating liquors

lock in a pub kept open illegally past licensing hours to everyone's delight

LV luncheon vouchers, which can be exchanged for meals and groceries at participating restaurants and shops; LVs are provided by some employers as part of one's salary

punt Irish word for pound (£) (like American "buck" for dollar)

rucksack backpack

Semtex a Czechoslovakian-made explosive material used in many homemade IRA bombs

serviette dinner napkin

sick puke, vomit, *as a noun*, as in "Is that sick on your shoes?"

sledge sled

stone fourteen pounds (weight measurement)

tied house a pub owned by a single brewery

Tipp-Ex white out, liquid paper, correction fluid

torch flashlight

zed the letter *z*

COCKNEY VOCABULARY

Rhyming slang developed for use in the markets in London's East End, so that the merchants could communicate with each other without their customers understanding them. A true Cockney must have been born within earshot of "Bow Bells," the bells of the Bow church.

Cockney Example

I was robin hood at the fireplace checking my wallet, I had only a big ben for the night out. I left the trouble and strife in the dan dare watching the goggle box, and went to the rub a dub dub to meet my grates. They were a bit andy pandy with their dabs and soon got into a turkish delight with a tea leaf from over the river. Someone dog and boned the Old Bill so we were off on our plates of meat, down a bow and arrow alley and I slipped in the bread and butter.

I got home and had a cup of rosie lee, went up the apples and pears, showed percy the porcelain and took a butcher's hook at the bin lids, got into the lump of lead and was tom dick all over the trouble and strife.

English Translation

I stood at the fireplace checking my wallet, and had only £10 for the night out. I left the wife in the chair watching the television, and went to the pub to meet my mates. They were a bit handy with their fists and soon got into a fight with a thief from over the river. Someone phoned the police so we were off on our feet, down a narrow alley and I slipped in the gutter.

I got home and had a cup of tea, went up the stairs to the toilet, took a look at the kids, got into bed and was sick all over the wife.

—Jörgen Dyer

Cockney Vocabulary

andy pandy handy	**lump of lead** bed
apples and pears stairs	**mum and dad** mad
bin lids kids	**pen and ink** stink
bow and arrow narrow	**plates of meat** feet
Brahms and Liszt pissed (drunk)	**robin hood** stood
bread and butter gutter	**rosie lee** tea
big ben ten, £10	**rub a dub dub** pub
dan dare chair	**tea leaf** thief
dog and bone telephone	**tom dick** sick
grates mates	**trouble and strife** wife
have a butcher's hook have a look	**turkish delight** fight

THE WELSH LANGUAGE

Welsh is a Celtic language, separate and distinct from English, singsong and gloppy, with plenty of hisses and guttural spits. Welsh shares its Celtic heritage with Scots Gaelic, Irish Gaeilge, Cornish (in southwest England), and the language of Brittany in northwestern France. The language is part of the national identity of Wales, and some students, especially those in the north of Wales, attend schools where it's the only spoken tongue. If you go to a college of the University of Wales, make Welsh friends, or travel through the country and try to read signs, you'll definitely come across the language. Although the following list will give you a sense of the range of vocabulary you'll encounter if you're visiting the country, students spending an academic term should purchase a complete phrasebook.

All colleges of the University of Wales require signs posted in both English *(saesneg)* and Welsh *(cymraeg)*.

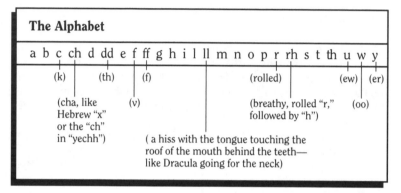

The Alphabet

a b c ch d dd e f ff g h i l ll m n o p r rh s t th u w y

(k)　　(th)　　(f)　　　　　　　　(rolled)　　　　(ew)　(er)

(cha, like　　(v)　　　　　　　　(breathy, rolled "r,"　　(oo)
Hebrew "x"　　　　　　　　　　followed by "h")
or the "ch"
in "yechh")　　(a hiss with the tongue touching the
roof of the mouth behind the teeth—
like Dracula going for the neck)

A *circumflex (^)* or *little roof* over a vowel extends the length of time you hold that vowel. Some common letter combinations and pronunciations:

Welsh Spelling	Pronounced
oe	oy
ei	ay
ae	ay
wy	oo-ee
si	shi

For practice, try pronouncing the name of this tiny Welsh town:

Llan-fair-pwll-gwyn-gyll-goger-y-chwyrn-
llan vire pooll gwin gill goger er queern
Saint-Mary-pool-white-hazelnut tree-near-the-rapid

drobwll-llan-tysilio-gogo-goch
drobooll llan dersilio gogo goch
whirlpool-Saint-Tisilio-cave-red

Useful Welsh Vocabulary
(Phonetic spellings provided for greetings only)

Greetings

bore da (boray da) Good morning
croeso i chi (croyso ee-'ch'-ee)
You're welcome
da boch (da boch) Good-bye
diolch yn fawr (dee-olch un vower)
Thank you very much
esgusodwch fi (eskeesodoch vee)
Excuse me
nos da (nos da) Good night
Sut ydech chi? (Siddach chi) How
are you?

Places

bws stesion bus station
bwyty café, restaurant
Cymru Wales
Ffordd Allan Way Out; Exit
glan bank
gwesty inn, hotel
heol fawr high street, main street
Iwerddon Ireland
llan sacred ground, saint, church,
parish, village, town
llety efrydwyr hostel
Lloegr England
siop lyfrau bookshop
Snowdonia Ring North Welsh
mountain-ringed region that's
supposedly never been conquered
by the English (includes college
at Bangor)
swyddfa'r pôst post office
tafarn pub, tavern
tai hâf summer homes, likely to
be razed by the Meibion Glyndwr
trén stesion train station
toiledau toilets

Yr Alban Scotland
Yr Unol Daleithiau United States

University

adloniant ents, entertainments
astudio to study
clwb rygbi rugby club
efrydiau studies
llyfrgell library
myfyrwyr student
neuadd hall of residence
prifysgol university
Undeb y Myfyrwyr Student Union
**Undeb Cenedlaethol Myfyrwyr
Cymru (UCMC)** National Union
of Students,Wales (NUS Wales)
Urdd y Myfyrwyr Guild of Students

People

Dewi Sant Saint David, the patron saint of Wales
dynion men
gogs South Welsh term for the
North Welsh ("gogledd" means
north)
heddlu police
hwntws North Welsh term for the
SouthWelsh(means"down below")
Meibion Glyndwr "Sons of Glendower," Welsh nationalist group
merched women
myfyrwyr students
myfyrwyr tramor overseas students
Owain Glyndwr (Owine Glendoo-
er) famous Welsh historical figure who booted out the English
in 1404

Plaid Cymru Welsh Nationalist Party (wants greater autonomy as a separate nation within the European Community)
saeson Saxons; English people

Things

Hen Wlad Fy Nhadau "The Land of My Fathers," the Welsh national anthem
Harlech TV (HTV) Welsh independent TV network
Pobl y Cwm "People of the Valley," South Welsh soap opera on S4C
Sianel Pedwar Cymru (S4C) Welsh Channel 4

Expressions

am ddim free
ar agor open
ar gau closed
ar werth for sale
Ble mae'r dafarn? Where's the pub?
Ble mae'r ty bach? Where's the toilet?
Cau dy geg! Shut up!
Cymru Am Byth! Wales Forever!
Iechyd da (yechh eeda) Cheers!, Good Health! (when toasting someone)
Nadolig Llawen! Happy Christmas!
Penblwydd Hapus Happy Birthday
uffern dân hell on fire!, damn!
Wyt ti'n siarad saesneg? Do you speak English?

The Calendar

The following is a list of major holidays and events in Britain and Ireland. U.S. and Canadian holidays are included because it's often difficult to remember them when you're studying overseas.

NOTE: A *bank holiday* is an official, national holiday in Britain and Ireland.

JANUARY

Chinese New Year (in January or February)
January 1: **New Year's Day** (U.S., Canada, Britain, Ireland)
January 2: **Bank Holiday** (unless New Year's falls on a Sunday, in which case it's celebrated on January 3; Scotland)
Bank Holiday (first Monday in January; Britain)
January 15: **Martin Luther King, Jr.'s Birthday** (U.S.)
January 25: **Burns Night** (celebrates the birth of the great Scottish poet, Robert Burns. You eat tatties and neeps while a kilted man walks around playing the bagpipes and another one follows him with a haggis, reciting Burns's "To A Haggis" and slicing off portions; Scotland)

FEBRUARY

Ash Wednesday (start of Lent)
February 2: **Groundhog Day** (U.S.)
February 14: **Valentine's Day** (U.S., Canada, Britain, Ireland)
President's Day (the Monday following the third weekend; U.S.)

MARCH

Mothering Sunday (the fourth Sunday in Lent, the fourth Sunday after Ash Wednesday); **buy your cards now**—you won't find them in May; Britain and Ireland's version of Mother's Day
Oxford and Cambridge Boat Race (rowing up the Thames from Putney to Mortlake; intense rivalry, fancy clothes, yuppie drunkenness; March or April)
March 1: **St. David's Day** (patron saint of Wales; Wales)
March 17: **St. Patrick's Day** (patron saint of Ireland; U.S., Canada, and Ireland, although the biggest celebrations are in Boston, Philadelphia, Chicago, and New York)
Good Friday (two days before Easter Sunday; March or April)
Easter Sunday (March or April)

APRIL

Grand National (horse racing in Aintree, Liverpool; Britain)
Irish Grand National (horse racing in the Republic of Ireland)

MAY

Glasgow's Mayfest (first two weeks; Scotland)
Brighton Festival (first two weeks; England)
Hay-on-Wye International Literary Festival (for one weekend; Wales)
Bath Festival (for two weeks from May to June; England)
May Day (the first Monday; Britain)
Mother's Day (second Sunday; U.S., Canada)
May 19: **Armed Forces Day** (U.S.)
May 21: **Victoria Day** (Canada)
Memorial Day (the last Monday; U.S.)
Spring Bank Holiday (the last Monday; Britain)

JUNE

Glastonbury Festival (major hippie gathering in Glastonbury, England,
supposed sight of the Holy Grail; plenty of mysticism, music, hash)
Henley Regatta (a major social occasion; June or July; Britain)
June 3-6: **Derby Horse Races** (in Epsom, Surrey, a colorful race known
for its fairs, gypsies, huge crowds, and compulsive betting; the best-known
flat race; Britain)
June 16-19: **Royal Ascot** (horse race in Berkshire, attended by the Queen;
England)
June Holiday (first Monday; Republic of Ireland)
Trooping the Colours (official celebration of the Queen's birthday, on the
nearest Saturday to June 11; Britain)
Father's Day (second Sunday; U.S., Canada, Britain, Ireland)
June 14: **Flag Day** (U.S.)
June 21: **Summer Solstice** (the start of summer, when druids and travelers
rush police lines around Stonehenge near Salisbury, England)
Wimbledon (you *can* get tickets: get there early and queue up; end of June
to early July)

JULY

July 1: **Canada Day** (Canada)
July 4: **American Independence Day** (U.S.)
July 12: **Orangeman's Day Holiday** (Northern Ireland)
Dublin International Folk Festival (for three days; Ireland)
The Proms (July to August at the Royal Albert Hall in London; annual
series of performances by orchestras from around the world; England)

AUGUST

Welsh National Eisteddfod (celebration of Welsh traditions of storytelling
and song held alternately in the north and south of the country each year;
for one week; Wales)
Edinburgh International Festival and Fringe Festival (premier interna-
tional arts festival and concurrently run, self-described "fringe festival":
drama, exhibits, performance; for three weeks; Scotland)
Edinburgh Military Tattoo (military pageant on the grounds of Edinburgh
Castle; for three weeks; Scotland)
Summer Bank Holiday (first Monday; Ireland and Scotland)
Summer Bank Holiday (last Monday; England and Wales)

All-Ireland Fleadh (national traditional Irish music festival, held in a different part of the country each year on the last weekend in August; Ireland)

SEPTEMBER

Labor Day (first Monday; U.S.)
Rosh Hashanah (New Year according to the Jewish Calendar)
Yom Kippur (tenth day after the Jewish New Year)

OCTOBER

Gaelic Mod (Highland and island choral group competition held in a different part of the country each year; Scotland)
October 8: **Thanksgiving** (Canada)
Columbus Day (second Monday; U.S.)
Guinness Jazz Festival (for three days; Cork, Ireland)
October 28: **October Holiday** (Republic of Ireland)
October 31: **Halloween, All Hallow's Eve** (U.S., Canada, Ireland—not a big holiday in Britain)

NOVEMBER

Belfast Arts Festival (based at Queens University of Belfast, whose lecture halls become nightclubs and theaters; events, music, drama, exhibits at venues all over the city; the whole month; Northern Ireland)
London to Brighton Veteran Car Run (classic cars take to the road; first Sunday; England)
November 5: **Guy Fawkes Day** (annual celebration of the demise of Guy Fawkes, a Catholic who attempted to blow up Protestant Parliament with gunpowder ("The Gunpowder Plot") in the seventeenth century; in some small South England towns, the celebration includes costumes, torch-lit marches, liberally tossed firecrackers, and a burning in effigy of the Pope and his minions; Britain, mostly England)
Election Day (first Tuesday after the first Monday; U.S.)
Lord Mayor's Show (second Saturday; the Lord Mayor rides through the city in a golden coach; London)
November 11: **Veteran's Day** (U.S.)
November 11: **Remembrance Day** (Canada)
Remembrance Sunday (commemorates the end of World Wars I and II; the Sunday closest to November 11; Britain)

Thanksgiving (fourth Thursday; U.S.)
November 30: **St. Andrew's Day** (patron saint of Scotland; Scotland)

DECEMBER

Hanukkah
December 24: **Christmas Eve**
December 25: **Christmas Day**
December 26: **Boxing Day** (the day after Christmas, when servants traditionally received boxes of leftover food; Canada, Britain)
December 26: **St. Stephen's Day** (Republic of Ireland)
December 31: **New Year's Eve**
December 31: **Hogmanay** (New Year's Eve in Scotland; you say "Happy Hogmanay!" instead of "Happy New Year!"; from an Old French word meaning the last day of the year; Scotland)

APPENDIX E

Transportation and Travel

THE LONDON UNDERGROUND ZONE 1 CENTRAL AREA

The following map is meant as a rough guide to London's extensive underground system. All tube stations are marked; however, not all are named and not all tube lines are included. Complete maps are available from any tube station.

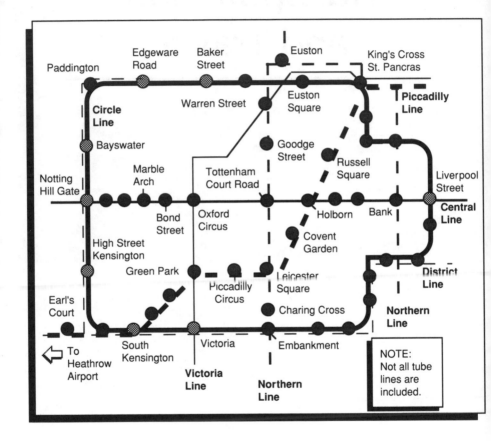

Paddington · Edgeware Road · Baker Street · Euston · King's Cross St. Pancras

Circle Line · Warren Street · Euston Square · Piccadilly Line

Bayswater · Goodge Street · Russell Square

Notting Hill Gate · Marble Arch · Tottenham Court Road · Liverpool Street · Central Line

Bond Street · Oxford Circus · Holborn · Bank

High Street Kensington · Covent Garden

Green Park · Leicester Square · District Line

Earl's Court · Piccadilly Circus · Charing Cross · Northern Line

To Heathrow Airport · South Kensington · Victoria · Embankment

Victoria Line · Northern Line

NOTE:
Not all tube lines are included.

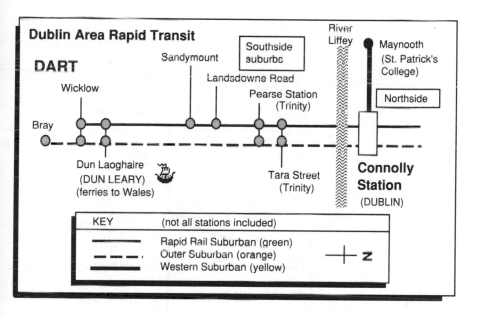

HITCHING IN BRITAIN

For more information on hitching, see chapter 6. As noted there, the combinations most likely to win rides are a man and a woman, or two women; remember, a woman should never hitchhike alone.

- **To the M1:** Jubilee line tube to Kilburn Station, then bus #16 north to Staples Corner. The roundabout there routes cars to the M1.

- **To the M2:** Bus #53 to Blackheath. Get off along Shooters Hill Road and walk to the roundabout.

- **To the M3:** District line tube to Richmond Station. Walk along Twickenham Road to Chertsey Road, which intersects the M3.

- **To the M4:** District line tube to Chiswick Park. Turn right along Chiswick High Street, and it's a bit of a hike to the roundabout.

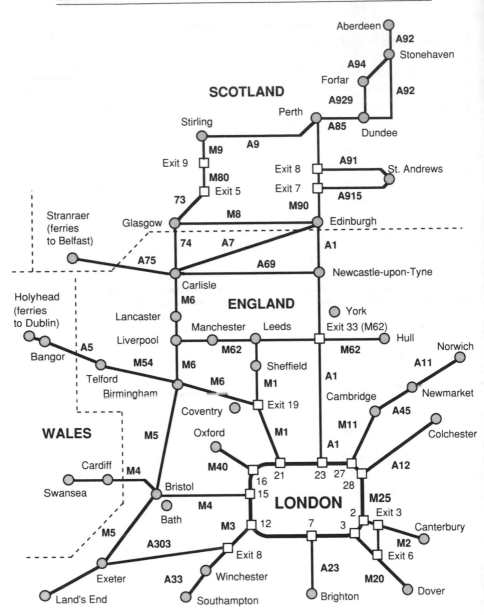

NOTE: a few of the *M-roads* (or motorways) leaving London off the M25 start as *A-roads* and don't become motorways until further on. Alternately, some of the roads beginning as M-roads turn into A-roads. In either case, the number remains the same unless indicated above.

HITCHING IN IRELAND

The roads are smaller, the competition keener, but the rides come quicker in the Green Isle. Hitching is a respected and oft-used form of transportation in a country without much of a rail system.

• **To Belfast:** Take airport bus from Busáras to the roundabout by Dublin Airport, on the N1.

• **To Cork/Kerry:** Take bus #51 from Fleet Street and get off at Newlands Cross, on the Naas Road (the N7). Join the queue!

• **To Galway/Donegal:** Take bus #66 from Middle Abbey Street to Maynooth, on the N4.

• **To Waterford/Rosslare:** Take bus #45 from Poolbeg Street and ask to be let off at Wexford Rd.

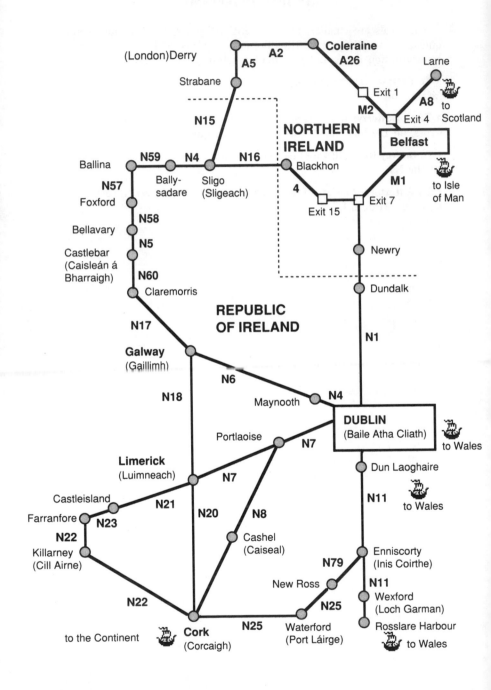

YOUTH HOSTELS

Contact the following organizations for the most current information about obtaining a hostel card and guide:

An Óige, Irish Youth Hostel Association
39 Mounjoy Square South
Dublin 1
Republic of Ireland
tel. (01) 363111

American Youth Hostels, Inc. (AYH)
Post Office Box 37613
Washington, DC 20013-7613
United States
tel. (202) 783-6161

Canadian Hosteling Association
1600 James Naismith Drive
Gloucester, Ontario K1B 5N4
Canada
tel. (416) 363-0697

England and Wales Hosteling Association (YHA)
Trevelyan House
8 St. Stephen's Hill
St. Albans, Herts AL1 2DY
England
tel. (0727) 55215

Kinlay House
Christchurch
2/12 Lord Edward Street   Shandon
Dublin 2   Cork City
tel. (01) 679-6644   tel. (021) 508-966

Scottish Youth Hostels Association (SYH)
7 Glebe Crescent
Stirling FK8 2JA
Scotland
tel. (0786) 51181

Youth Hostel Association of Northern Ireland
56 Bradbury Place
Belfast BT7 1RU
Northern Ireland
tel. (232) 324733

TRAVEL AGENCIES

Contact the following agencies to discover the cheapest flights and travel buys. In general you must present your student ID to receive any special rates. For more information on flight arrangements, see chapter 6.

In the United States:

Council Travel
c/o Council on International Educational Exchange (CIEE)
205 East 42nd Street
New York, NY 10017
United States
tel. (212) 661-1414

CIEE publishes the *Student Travel Catalog* ($1) listing all their travel offices, plus information on work, study, and travel abroad

International Student Exchange Flights
5010 East Shea Boulevard, Suite A104
Scottsdale, AZ 85254
United States
tel. (602) 951-1177

STA Travel
7202 Melrose Avenue
Los Angeles, CA 90046
tel. (213) 934-8722; (800) 777-0112

STA Travel is the leading budget agency in Britain, found on several university campuses (Birmingham, Brunel, Kent, Loughborough, etc.)

In Canada

Travel Cuts
171 College Street
Toronto, Ontario M5T 1P7
Canada
tel. (416) 979-2406

In Britain and Ireland:

Council Travel
Tube: Oxford Circus
28A Poland Street
London W1V 3DB
United Kingdom
tel. (071) 437-7767

Iarnród Éireann Travel Center

35 Lower Abbey Street	65 Patrick Street
Dublin 1	Cork
Republic of Ireland	Republic of Ireland
tel. (01) 363-333	

London Student Travel
Tube: Victoria Station
52 Grosvenor Gardens
London SW1
United Kingdom
tel. (071) 730-3402; (071) 824-8099

STA Travel
Tube: South Kensington
74 & 86 Old Brompton Road
London SW7 3LQ
United Kingdom
tel. (071) 937-9921

Union of Students in Ireland Travel (USIT)
(along the River Liffey at O'Connell Bridge)
19-21 Aston Quay
O'Connell Bridge
Dublin 2
Ireland
tel. (01) 778117

USIT is the leading travel center in Ireland. Offers cheap flights, along with other budget travel and accommodation services (there's a notice board for flats in their main office). You'll find them at University College Cork and University College Galway, too.

COURIER AGENCIES

Contact the following companies to arrange for cheap courier flights. For U.S. companies, consult the Yellow Pages. See chapter 6 for more information.

Courier Travel Services (CTS)
Johnson House
Browells Lane
Feltham
Middlesex TW13 7EQ
tel. (081) 844-2626

Fly from London to New York, Boston, Los Angeles, Chicago, San Francisco, Houston, Dallas, Atlanta, Sydney, Paris, and other destinations

Nomad Courier Flights
224 Great West Road
Heston
Middlesex TW5 9AW
tel. (081) 570-9277

Fly from London to Los Angeles, Miami, New York, Montreal, Toronto, Vancouver, and other cities

Polo Express
208 Epsom Square
Heathrow Airport
Hounslow, Middlesex TW6 2BL
tel. (081) 759-5699

Fly from London to Boston, Miami, New York, Philadelphia, Seattle, Washington D.C., Montreal, Abu Dhabi, Amsterdam, Athens, Auckland, Dublin, etc.; dress code for couriers: men must wear ties

MAJOR FERRY OPERATORS

The following is list of main office contact addresses for information and bookings:

• **B&I Line** (Reliance House, Water Street, Liverpool L2 8TP, tel. 051-227-3131)

• **Sealink British Ferries** (Charter House, Park Street, Ashford, Kent TN24 8EX, tel. (0233)-647033)

• **Belfast Car Ferries** (North Brocklebank Dock, Bootle, Merseyside, Liverpool L20 1DB, tel. 051-922-6234)

• **P&O European Ferries** (Cairnryan near Stranraer, Wigtownshire, Scotland, tel. 05812-276)

• **Sealink Scotland** (Sea Terminal, Stranraer, Dumfries & Galloway DG9 8EL, tel. 0776-2262)

• **Swansea Cork Ferries** (Swansea Ferryport, Kings Dock, Swansea SA1 8RN, tel. 0792-456116)

IRELAND

BRITAIN

Larne
Northern Ireland
(near Belfast)

2.5 hours
—————————————————
Townsend Thoreson (05812) 276
Sealink (0776) 2262

Stranraer
Scotland

Belfast
Northern Ireland

9 hours
—————————————————
Belfast Car Ferries (051) 922-6234

Liverpool
England

Dublin
Republic of Ireland

3.5 hours
—————————————————
B&I Line: Dublin (01) 724711
Holyhead (0407) 50222

Holyhead
Wales

Dun Laoghaire
(DUN LEARY)
Republic of Ireland
(near Dublin: see
Trains chapter for
DART connections
to city center)

3.5 hours
—————————————————
Sealink: Dublin (01) 808844
Dun Laoghaire (01) 774206
Holyhead (0407) 762039

Holyhead
Wales

Rosslare
Republic of Ireland
(near Wexford)

3.5 hours
—————————————————
B&I Line: Rosslare (053) 33311
Fishguard (0348) 872881
Sealink: Rosslare (053) 33115
Fishguard (0348) 872881

Fishguard
Wales

Cork
Republic of Ireland

14 hours
—————————————————
Swansea Cork Ferries:
Cork (021) 271166
Swansea (0792) 456116

Swansea
Wales

MAJOR BRITAIN-IRELAND FERRY ROUTES

NOTE: Although you probably won't be asked for it, remember to bring your passport in case you are pulled aside by customs control.